Praise for *Let's Shut Out the*

"An unpretentious autobiography in the form of about a dozen well-focused episodes from the author's life, *Let's Shut Out the World* continues the narrative, and even more, the voice I liked so much in *Wild Animals I Have Known*. It's funny, wry, sad sometimes but never sour. While the stories of Kevin's hopelessly misfit life in hyper-religious West Texas were funny, the meat of the book for me came once the author moved to San Francisco. His beautifully written memories of a life lived in the heart of the gay ghetto and on the margin of respectability are exactly right—not portentous, not trivial. Any gay person would recognize Kevin's story, but guys in their 40s and up will feel it's their own life, only funnier, better written, and with more sex in it. It's a terrific book." —Reed Woodhouse, author of *Unlimited Embrace: A Canon of Gay Fiction*

"Reading Kevin Bentley's memoirs is like listening to an especially literate and funny friend tell you about his entertainingly deplorable past. Better him than me, I found myself thinking time and again. But that's true on two levels. I wouldn't want to have lived through a lot of what Bentley has, but I have to admit I couldn't have written about it nearly as beautifully either." —Ed Sikov, author of *On Sunset Boulevard: The Life and Times of Billy Wilder*

"These total-recall reminiscences, from boyhood in El Paso to full immersion in the San Francisco gay community, are such good reading and so evocative of their times they could go in a time capsule." —Katherine V. Forrest, Lambda Award-winning author of the Kate Delafield mystery series

Let's Shut Out the World

Let's Shut Out the World

Kevin
Bentley

Green Candy Press

Let's Shut Out The World
by Kevin Bentley
ISBN 1-931160-33-3

Published by Green Candy Press, www.greencandypress.com

Cover and interior design: Ian Phillips
Front cover photo: Copyright © Jack Slomovits, www.jackny.com
Author photo: Richard Morgenstein

Some proper names and details have been changed and in some cases composites created in these autobiographical essays to protect the privacy of living individuals.

"Six Crises of Bullmoose" first appeared in *The Man I Might Become: Gay Men Write About Their Fathers*, edited by Bruce Shenitz; "Slender" first appeared in *His 2: Brilliant New Fiction by Gay Writers*, edited by Robert Drake and Terry Wolverton; "Deeper Inside the Valley of Kings" first appeared in *Flesh and the Word 4: Gay Erotic Confessionals*, edited by Michael Lowenthal; "Do You Believe I Love You?" first appeared in *Bar Stories*, edited by Scott Brassart; "My Clementina" appeared in different versions in *Diseased Pariah News* and *POZ*; "Widow-Hopper" appeared in *Diseased Pariah News* and *Boyfriends from Hell: True Tales of Tainted Lovers, Disastrous Dates, and Love Gone Wrong*; "Chimayó" first appeared on beliefnet.com; "Suddenly" and "Moon of Monokoora" first appeared in *ZYZZYVA*.

Printed in Canada by Transcontinental Printing Inc.
Massively Distributed by P.G.W.

For Joyce

The sable divinity would not herself dwell with us always, but we could counterfeit her presence. At the first dawn of the morning we closed all the massy shutters of our old building; lighted a couple of tapers which, strongly perfumed, threw out only the ghastliest and feeblest of rays. By the aid of these we then busied our souls in dreams—reading, writing, or conversing, until warned by the clock of the advent of the true Darkness.

—Edgar Allan Poe, "The Murders in the Rue Morgue"

Contents

Six Crises of Bullmoose

My mother got leukemia the year before I turned forty, and the prognosis was grim. I hadn't been back to El Paso in thirteen years, and we hadn't been talking much for the last six, but now we talked—long phone calls about her condition, current events, and some awkward words of regret. "I'm sure you're going to make it, but I still want to come see you," I said.

"Wait," she said. "I have to talk to Daddy."

That had a sadly familiar ring. In the period after I'd first left home, when she and I were still in regular touch, she would call me from the back bedroom, her voice low so Daddy wouldn't hear. Critical conversations had often ended this way, with a follow-up call a day or two later to deliver the verdict.

No, my best friend couldn't stay over at the house during a brief trip home. No, they wouldn't loan me a modest amount of money against my dying lover's life insurance so we could afford cab rides to the doctor.

"Daddy says if we give you this money now it'll just be more next time—and then what if *you* get sick?"

I did go back that once, for a few days in the summer of 1982—a visit that made clear all I'd missed out on by making a life so far away. On my last evening we gathered for a backyard cookout. My older brother Randy arrived with his new, second wife, a peppy Filipina in a halter top and cha-cha heels, and popped open a Coors. My younger brother, Mark, who was still living at home, cranked up some country rock. Without warning, my father rushed out of the house, flushed, his fists clenched. "Turn down that goddamn music!" he snarled, and knocked over the boom box.

"Fuck you!" Mark abandoned the sizzling steaks, stomped to the driveway, and tore away from the house, tires screeching.

Randy slammed his beer on the patio, where it fizzed like a grenade. "You fucking asshole, why do you always have to spoil everything?" He headed for his truck, Tina wobbling after, her heels sinking into the grass.

My mother, who'd been making potato salad in the kitchen a few feet away, screamed, *"I hate you all!"*—which seemed a bit unfair, as I hadn't moved from my lawn chair or uttered a word—and slammed her bedroom door so loudly I expected to see the house collapse in on itself like a set in a Buster Keaton film. Flames were shooting wildly from the barbecue and I walked over and shut the lid.

Twenty minutes later, as I sat at the kitchen counter eating potato salad out of the serving bowl, and thinking about whom I might meet at the Castro Street Fair when I flew home to San Francisco the next day, my mother appeared, went into the garage, and returned. "Daddy's sitting in his car cleaning his rifle."

"I don't understand, is he going to asphyxiate himself or blow his head off?"

"You know I couldn't survive on just my salary, without his retirement," she said, loading the untouched dishes into the dishwasher.

Daddy. His relationship to us was more that of a spiteful and jealous sibling than the wise and heartwarming TV dads like Fred MacMurray on *My Three Sons* or Carl Betz on *The Donna Reed Show* we watched in disbelief. "Bullmoose," my mother called him when we were little: "King Bullmoose has spoken." What must have begun as a pet name was later uttered with sarcasm and resignation to the kind of bullying, indifferent authority he exercised.

I remember sitting weeping in a swing in our backyard while my father chased down the now-gangly Easter chicks we'd gotten at the dime store two weeks before and strangled them in their ludicrously half pink, half chicken-colored state, with pliers.

At Christmas, when the elaborately brown-paper-wrapped and twine-bound package arrived from his eccentric mother in Georgia, addressed to my brothers and me in her loopy nine-teenth-century handwriting, he'd open it up and smash or rip apart the contents. Granted they were oddly inappropriate gifts for children—chipped figurines, ancient sheet music—but still. Years later my mother told me, "Your father's mother caught him, you know, touching himself in the bathtub when he was a little boy so she whipped him with an egg turner and put

Tabasco sauce on his *potty-er.*"

Any remotely anthropomorphic toy I talked to, slept with, or tried to put outfits on, mysteriously disappeared. Half my childhood was spent in a grim battle to get my hands on a doll. An aunt gave me a Cecil the Sea Serpent toy for my fifth birthday: he was only a bendable plush green tube with goggly eyes and a gaping mouth at one end and red felt scales down his back, but he came with disguises—Sherlock Holmes cap and pipe, Zorro cape. My father observed me carefully tying the red cape around Cecil's neck, and the next day the toy had vanished. "I don't know, are you sure you looked in your toy chest?" he'd say. "Maybe you left it outside and a dog carried it away." For a while puppets escaped his scrutiny. Soon I had a shelf full of hand puppets with which I privately acted out complicated soap opera plots: Dopey the Dwarf, Lambchop, a furry monkey. The best was a Mattel Dishonest John, in a black gown and black villain's hat, which uttered, at the pull of a string, "*Yaah*-ah-ah!" and a withering, "Go soak your *head!*" But someone was watching. When we unpacked after a move several states away to an Army base in Alabama, not one puppet could be found. "Movers—those jackasses! They always lose one box!" my father said.

His occasional staged attempts at fatherly hijinks invariably went awry. He'd stretch his six-foot-four length down on the carpet and offer my older brother a quarter if he could make him laugh or say "uncle," and a rollicking wrestling match would ensue. Once, probably five years old, summoned to make the same attempt, I matter-of-factly reached for his testicles through the baggy slacks, and was angrily driven to my room in a hail of slaps and cuffs. "Don't you *ever* touch me there again!" he screeched, red-faced.

He used to poke his head into the bathroom when, as little boys, my older brother and I bathed together. "Be sure and use the washcloth and get it real clean—you know—*there*," he'd say in a weird tone, looking away, but gesturing to indicate we should skin our penises back and soap up the glans. Why would he say that, when we were circumcised? He entered the Army at eighteen completely ignorant; what he knew of sex and hygiene he'd learned in training films. I don't think he understood this particular regime was meant for men with foreskins.

May 1960: We're sitting at the kitchen table eating breakfast—Trix, Cocoa-Puffs—Randy, aged seven; me, four; and my mother, reading the paper in her housecoat. We can hear my father whistling as he shaves in the distant bathroom. There's been more tension than usual in the last few weeks. I've seen my mother, wearing a cornflower blue dress with a full skirt, wide belt, and large buttons I'll always associate with her unhappiness, standing in the dark hall, turned to the wall, her face in her hands, sobbing.

Her favorite part of the morning paper, which she turns to now, is the obits and legal notices. Her eye scans a column of type, halts. She drops the paper with a bloodcurdling scream, sweeps her plate, cup, and silverware off the table and crashing onto the floor, and runs from the room. My father's whistling pauses, continues.

I wouldn't learn the story behind this event till decades later. They'd been arguing about her third pregnancy. My father had secretly filed for divorce—it would go no further—and let her read it in the paper.

We're lying on our backs in the shallow plastic wading pool

in the far corner of the backyard, churning the water with our feet—Randy, our neighbor Cindy, and me. July 1962: I am six. Thirteen-year-old Cindy has only recently moved in down the block, and so far she has only made friends with younger kids like us. We kick to circulate the water in the hot afternoon sun, to shoo away the hovering bees from a neighbor's stacked hives, and to obscure our voices. My mother, who doesn't like Cindy and thinks it's odd she should spend so much time with two little boys, twitches the bathroom curtain aside to check up on us from time to time.

Cindy wants to see our penises. She'll show us her pussy, she says, if we'll go first. Randy grudgingly lifts the leg of his trunks and proffers a brief glimpse of puckered scrotum. Cindy peels back one side of her swimsuit and pinches out a plug of pink flesh. I am standing accommodatingly with my clammy suit around my ankles, when our father swoops down on us shouting, and drags us both into the house.

We had done something so horrible it couldn't be named. We'd been slapped occasionally for back talk or misbehavior, our legs and arms flailed at with the fly swatter by my mother, and, for the most serious crimes, subjected to the elaborate ritual of punishment with my father's belt. You had to unzip and pull down your pants, leaving underwear in place. My father loomed above as he silently unbuckled and swished his tooled leather cowboy belt out of the belt loops. He began with the belt doubled over, but if you tried to straighten up or block the strokes with your arm, he'd become enraged and use the full length, which could mean getting hit with the buckle.

This time, shut in the next room, terrified, I heard the belt ritual quickly escalate to something more violent, with my father shouting angrily, and my brother screaming with surprised pain. Even my mother was frightened, slapping her palms on the locked door and crying, "For God's sake, Max, that's enough!"

"You'll be next," I'd been told. I lay huddled trembling for the next several hours, expecting my beating each time footsteps approached the door. But when my father finally came to get me, it was for dinner. "You've had your punishment," he said smugly.

July 1967: We're living in an Army housing duplex at Fort Campbell, Kentucky. My father, who's never played a sport of any kind, informs me that I'm going to spend several days a week after school shooting hoops with Corporal Byrd, the young officer next door. It's my pudgy period. I hate PE and would sooner die than take off my shirt in public. My father has told us at dinner how, when their outfit had to cross a river on a wilderness survival course, Corporal Byrd stripped off his clothes and carried them across on his head. Corporal Byrd has a basketball hoop in his backyard. He's short and muscular, with a beak-like nose and a high forehead, and he plays basketball in a pair of black trunks with the white band of a jock strap riding up in back. He insists I take off my shirt. "What's the matter, are you a girl or something?" he says. When I throw the ball it goes nowhere near the hoop. It's a hot summer evening and I'm sweating; Corporal Byrd is drenched and reeking. He stands behind me, his body pressing closely, laces his fingers through mine, and ejects the ball out of my hands and through the hoop.

In this and other pungent and excruciating memories of gender awkwardness and homosexual inklings, why is it that my father is always present, lurking just at the edge of the frame, accuser and provoker, causing precisely the opposite of the effect he intended? *His* body repels me, but just to the side of him are those other enlisted men strutting in the shower at the base pool or buying cartons of condoms at the PX; posing shirtless, suntanned, and hairy-chested with their arms thrown over each other's shoulders in his Vietnam photos; swimming naked across a river with clothes piled on their heads. He leers from the periphery of these scenes no matter how I try to scissor him out.

Haircuts were critical to my father's authority. With the advent of the Beatles our dislike of trips to the Army base barber shop intensified, but every three weeks we were ordered to the car and driven to the Vitalis-charged bastion of masculinity where, amid worn stacks of *Argosy* and *Armed Forces Gazette,* a beefy bald man with woolly forearms and tattooed biceps brusquely shaved our heads to tidy burrs. This routine required our being pulled from our sickbeds speckled and scabby with chicken pox; my mother shrieked when we returned with open sores on our scalps and blood trickling down the backs of our necks. On one of these resentment-filled drives to the base barber shop, when Randy and I were thirteen and ten, he said, embarrassed and insinuating at the same time, "Um, you may be waking up and finding your pajamas stuck to you with something like Elmer's Glue." We remained silent.

Always, at any bus or train station, park, or movie theater, there were his ominous warnings about the men's room, and the men in black raincoats who'd "do bad things to you." I dreamt often of these faceless men in slick black raincoats abducting me, tucked into their pockets naked and hairless as a joey.

He was sent to Vietnam twice, and then to Germany for two years, and when he came home after the last of these long absences, his authority had irrevocably eroded. The first time he tried to make us get haircuts my older brother ran out the back door, vaulted over a fence, and didn't come back for two days. My father had taken an early retirement and stayed out of work for a long, uncomfortable time, hanging around the house drinking Carlo Rossi jug wine from colored plastic juice glasses, watching Spanish-language *Sesame Street* on TV and talking back to Big Bird and Cookie Monster.

In April of 1975, age nineteen, after a jolting four months living with a gang of dope buddies at an apartment near the local campus of the University of Texas I was attending, I moved back home.

My younger brother had moved into my old bedroom, so I had to take the cheery canary-yellow study next to my parents' room. My doper pals didn't call, but then I'd turned my back on them. My few straight friends from high school had fallen away since graduation. Amid the press-board furniture, dusty plastic flower arrangements, and gold carpeting, I tumbled backward into lonely adolescence. Several misguided crushes and grudging sex acts with stoned straight pals had taught me I was indeed queer; how was I going to make new friends now?

I was sulking in my room one night when my mother slipped in wearing the housecoat she'd sewn out of bright orange beach towels, and shut the door. "I just hate to see you so unhappy," she said, staring at the carpet and balling up a battered Kleenex in her fist, her voice quavering and soaring toward tears. "I don't *understand*. Is it drugs? Did Wayne get you hooked on pot?" Wayne was one of the straight pals I'd fallen in love with.

"Wayne didn't do anything to me!" I wailed. "I love him, and he doesn't love *me!*"

I cried inconsolably and my mother, who I hadn't touched in years, came forward and held me stiffly, patting my back, saying, "Hush, hush, you don't mean that...."

My father had always been a master eavesdropper, picking up extensions, lurking around corners. In this case, he'd listened at the door. As soon as my mother pulled out of the driveway the next morning, he appeared in my doorway, eczema-riddled jowls red and quivering, like some dense but dangerous boogie from *The Hobbit*.

"You'd better not bring any of your little queer buddies around here again, you got that? I won't have fairies in this house. If you want to associate with fairies, you'd better find somewhere else to live."

The last place I'd found to live hadn't worked out all that well. I didn't have my degree yet, and I was too stoned and thin-skinned to walk out and go to work at KFC. I would just have to kill myself.

My father was headed out for the day to attend a job seminar, but he waited to make sure I left for class. I got in my car and drove a few blocks away, parked, and waited till I saw him drive by, fussily adjusting his side-mirror. Then I drove to a 7-11 and bought a bottle of Boone's Farm Strawberry Hill wine and a bottle of Extra Strength Anacin and returned to the house. I locked myself in my room, pulling the bed out from the wall and into the center of the room to make a sort of bier.

Contemplating death as I gulped down the grainy tablets, I searched for a Gothic feeling, and could do no better than the Styrofoam tombs and crepe-paper hell flames of *Dark Shadows*, the horror soap I used to watch after school in the sixth grade that made fatal love seem so stupefyingly turgid. I put my *Dark Shadows* sound track album on the stereo, swallowed the rest of the Anacin and wine, and sank back among the crashing waves at Collingwood.

That was the plan, anyway. Hadn't I seen umpteen public service commercials where absent-minded drinkers died in their easy chairs with brandy snifters at their elbows after mixing booze and pills? Wouldn't sixty Anacin and a bottle of wine be as deadly? I felt queasy and anxious, and my ears began to ring painfully. Instead of drifting off to oblivion, I felt my heart racing and skipping alarmingly. I sat up and started to gag.

"That was a pretty *stupid* thing to do. I oughta pump your stomach just so you know what it feels like—but I think I'll let you puke every goddamn one of those aspirins up instead. What an idiot!" The intern walked away, stopping to say something to an orderly in blue scrubs, who glanced back over his shoulder, smirking. Randy, who traveled with a local rock band and was currently crashing in the little studio in back of our house, had driven me out to the Army hospital after I banged on his door and woke him, weeping and retching. "There's always another sunrise to see," he'd told me, beating out a drum solo on the hot steering wheel. In the emergency room, I drained the paper cupful of purple gel I'd been given, and began vomiting into a dirty mop bucket.

Later, I sat propped up on pillows in front of the TV on my parents' king-size bed, my mother holding cool wash-cloths to my brow and emptying my plastic bucket, counting the half-dissolved pills. My grandmother had come over, and she sat looking nervously away from me, tisking and shaking her head. She'd grown up on a dirt farm outside Abilene, wore faded wash-dresses, and always smelled comfortingly of Dentyne. "Why in the world would you want to do some-thing like this to your Mama?" she said mournfully, giving me a feeble pinch. "Why'd you want to go and be so *horsey?*"

Then I heard my father coming in the front door whistling, and I saw my mother's face harden as she rushed out to intercept him. I heard her voice rising angrily, and I let my head fall back while Grandma wiped my mouth with a clean towel.

I was reborn, though it took two more years to fully kick off the chrysalis. Several false starts later, I moved to San Francisco, where, as my mother correctly pointed out, "there are other people like you."

The next time I called my mother in the hospital, the faint, ill voice said, "You better not come—Daddy says you can't. See, I'm immune suppressed because of the chemo and Daddy says if you came I could get, *you know...*" She died a few days later. My father dug up her garden, emptied the house of everything associated with my mother and their children, and went to sev-eral mixers at a nearby church he'd never attended till then, where he met, and promptly married, a blonde widow.

The day before I hastily left home for good in 1977, my

father tackled me in the bright orange and gold kitchen as I came sailing in from a night out with a GI from a South El Paso gay bar, the Pet Shop. He was squeezing me from behind in some kind of makeshift wrestling grip, a sickening echo of my previous night's grappling, trying to pry my car keys out of my clenched fist.

"Mom!" I yelled. "Dad's gone insane! Call the police!" I could see her through the crimped orange café curtains, aiming the garden hose at a bed of petunias, hearing, not wanting to hear.

That's where I'm leaving them now: my mother flooding the flower box, straining not to hear, wishing it would all go away; Bullmoose red and choking with hatred. That's where I've left them.

Slender

Seventh-grade boys were uniformly shrimpy, but many of the girls had already assumed adult proportions—girls like Dina Potter: tall, with hairdos and hose, go-go boots and fur coats. Giantesses armored in harlequin glasses and padded bras, they chuffed around the gravel schoolyard in cliques, posing for high school guys who drove by honking and catcalling, and chanting quietly beside boys like me, *fairy fairy fairy*. I asked my older brother Randy what that meant. "Oh, a fairy's a male whore," he told me.

I made a serious misjudgment on Valentine's Day, when I slipped a love note wrapped around a rubbery troll doll I'd crafted in my Mattel Thingmaker into the pocket of Dina Potter's vast rabbit fur coat and sat back coolly at my desk to await her response, dreamily writing *Kevin 'n' Dina* in loopy cursive strokes across my binder.

"Eeeeeek!" Her melodramatic shriek got everyone's

attention. "Oh God—look what that *fag* put in my coat!" Mr. Striber, a troubled Mormon with a facial tic, made me go outside the cottage (a flimsy-walled overflow classroom up on cinderblocks) and stand for the rest of the afternoon with my nose in a circle he drew just out of reasonable reach. I knew then that the best I could hope for was the speedy arrival of summer and my chance to reinvent myself while everyone forgot about my humiliation.

Happily for me, an overweight, dull-normal kid named Karl Brent attracted the most virulent attention. He wore a black raincoat buttoned up to his chin in all weather and carried a monogrammed briefcase, which was one of the things about him that made me uncomfortable—surely it was only a matter of time before someone would point out that he and I shared the same initials? Karl entered the playground every day whistling and swinging his briefcase, his equally unpopular little sister Mona (who wore fifties-style starched petticoats that stuck out from her body and molded corkscrew curls) holding his hand, and every day he'd be tripped and jumped and kicked and punched and made to eat dirt while Mona ran for the principal, the briefcase usually ending up on the roof or thrown in front of traffic.

Then Karl Brent made his bad lot worse with one simple and fateful slipup. He sucked Troy Sager's dick. Troy Sager was a hood who lived with his mother in an apartment over the Hondo Cocktail Lounge, where she worked nights. He was tall and willowy, with mean dark eyes and a long, elegant, pointy nose. He wore a ripped jean jacket and was said to carry a switchblade. He was often absent for days at a time, sent up to the D-Home. One day Troy was seen showing Karl his knife in a far corner of the playground, and for a week or so they hung out together, dumbfounding everyone. Then Karl ditched class with Troy one day and went to his apartment, and the next day Troy let it be known that Karl had sucked his dick.

When the news broke, 7-A reached a point of near hysteria. Nobody was working, notes were flying, and Mr. Striber was beside himself. A crony of Dina Potter's got up to use the pencil sharpener, stopped in front of Karl, and spit in his face. I was palming a note from someone at just the moment Mr. Striber spun around from the blackboard, and he dragged me outside the cottage by my shirt collar, slamming me up against the thin metal wall.

Mr. Striber was a broad-shouldered man whose starched white shirts were always sweat-darkened in a wide circle around the armpits by midmorning. He was probably under thirty, and he'd have been sexy if he weren't such an asshole. Married, with several small children, he flirted tempestuously all day long with Tony Buck, an up-and-coming jock. When I wore my trendy Indian moccasins to class he sent me out to run two laps backward around the track, sneering, "I'll run those squaw shoes off you!" Tony, on the other hand, was subjected to daily mock-serious corporal punishments for his antics. "Tony, my stick's just *itching* for your butt today!"

"I want to know what's going on in there," Mr. Striber said leaning over me, one arm propped on the wall beside my head, pale blue eyes bulging. "Why is everyone throwing things at Karl Brent?"

"I don't know," I lied, naturally. "Something everyone says he did...."

"What does everyone say Karl did?"

"He went to Troy Sager's house and—"

"What? *What did he do?*" He was right up in my face like

17

a drill sergeant, and suddenly I felt like I was confessing not what Karl may or may not have done, but what I knew I secretly wanted to do so bad it made me dizzy to even think about it.

"He sucked his dick!"

Mr. Striber's eyes bugged like a cartoon character's might, and his twitch, which made it seem absurdly as if he were winking in conspiracy ("Just kiddin'!") worked spastically. He had me by the shoulders and he gave me a great teeth-rattling shake with each word: "Don't-You-Ever-Let-Me-Hear-You-Utter-Such-Filth-Again! Do-You-Understand-Me? Do-You?"

The cottage creaked as my classmates sped back to their seats from the row of windows at which they'd been watching. I sat at my desk with my head throbbing where it had banged against the metal wall. As pencils scraped and my chastened neighbors took down the math problems Mr. Striber reeled off, I stared down at my writing hand, my lap, Karl's head buried in his arms on his desk, the sandstorm blowing against the windows. I noted all these things as if seeing them for the first time, as if I were an alien anthropologist just beamed down from Alpha Centauri. I was a stranger with a secret. I no longer recognized myself.

We didn't have to change into gym clothes yet (*dressing out,* Coach called it), but we had an hour-long PE period before lunch in which all the seventh-grade boys came together to do jumping jacks and sit-ups on the sticky blacktop, and then were sent off in teams to play football, basketball, or baseball, depending on the season. We hadn't had an organized phys ed class at my old school back on the Army base at Fort Rucker, Alabama, where at recess you could throw around a ball or sit in the shade and read, just as you chose. Till now, barring my father's few lame attempts to make me shoot baskets in the backyard, I'd completely avoided sports. Now, PE made me hate school and hate my life. In the bull pen of that one hot and awkward hour a day, my wits counted for nothing; my ignorance of the games, and my tendency to avoid a ball in motion, brought me only scorn.

The hours away from school were poisoned with dread of the next day's gauntlet. I read a sappy Scholastic paperback, *Craig and Joan: Two Lives for Peace*—a story about two teens who killed themselves with carbon monoxide because they were so upset about the Vietnam War and because their parents thought they were seeing too much of each other—and contemplated suicide in colored Magic Marker block printing in my diary. "I'd rather die than wrestle tomorrow." "If I shot myself in the foot, would I still have to play basketball?" It's true that these terse entries usually perked up by the last line. "Went to Kmart with Mom and bought the new Mama Cass album. Bye!"

El Paso is built on desert, and that couldn't be hidden, no matter how many sickly nonbearing mulberry trees people planted, no matter how many cement and rock walls were sculpted, breaking the yards and blocks into ugly, hot grids. The sand blew back in and drifted against everything in frequent sandstorms, and tumbleweeds lumbered down streets with names like Edgerock and Sandstone and lodged against dusty evergreens on front lawns. The desert was always in sight, always encroaching, ready to bury the tacky stucco ranch houses and leave only the twin horse heads atop the Bronco Drive-In poking out of the dunes

Slender

like "Ozymandias."

The playing field was a transitory landscape of dust devils and shifting dunes, the backstop having to be dug out regularly. One scorching morning near the end of the school year, I stood daydreaming so far outfield I could barely hear the crack of the bat hitting the ball, when Joey Carson summoned me. Joey was in 7-E, a class in which I knew no one, and I was vaguely aware that he lived a few blocks away from me, in a house that always made my mother flinch when we drove by because it looked so trashy: rusty van on the lawn, flaking paint. I knew he was considered weird, but not like Karl Brent—he was ignored, but nobody picked on him. He was short and wiry, and was said to be a good batter when he played, but he didn't bother. He wore black T-shirts, his father's old Army fatigue pants, and cheap black-framed glasses, and had clear olive skin and longish black hair.

On this day he was doing something typically outré: he'd buried himself, lying on his back in the sand piled against the schoolyard wall. "Hey, c'mere, help me with this. What're you waiting for, the ball to come this way?" I walked over. "C'mon—just push it up over my arms. Careful! Don't get it in my face, for fucksake!" I patted the sand down right up to his neck. "They used to bury people like this for torture, you know? I saw this movie once. They buried this guy up to his neck and put honey on his nostrils and then ants came and just ate his brains." I stood back. "Okay, now walk over me. Go ahead."

I put a foot gingerly above where his legs should be.

"No, c'mon, walk right on me." I stepped self-consciously up and down his buried torso.

"Okay, that's it, just stand there." I was standing on his crotch. "See? You're standing right on my *dick* and I don't feel a thing!" I heard a chorus of angry voices yelling my last name, and turned to see the ball whizzing and skipping along the ground. I ran off after it.

After that, Joey and I seemed to happen into each other often out pedaling our Stingray bikes around the neighborhood. When school let out for the summer, he started coming over and ringing the doorbell: "Wanna come out and ride?" We'd pump our bikes down hard-packed trails into the desert in the heat of the day, sweat-soaked, pulling wheelies and wiping out, exploring. We found junked cars, illicit trash dumps strewn with interesting items: caches of empty liquor bottles, and sun-warped skin magazines. Joey liked to talk about the Beatles and girls he wanted to fuck. "You ever tried that?" he asked, pointing to a wrinkled photo in one of our squirreled-away magazines. A heavily lipsticked woman in a black bra and panties was giving a blowjob to a red, disembodied penis.

"Nope," I lied, primly. Actually, I had first tried it with my friend Rick Watts in the fourth grade; he'd been sucking off his older brothers. We did it to each other for a while during a commercial break in *The Outer Limits*, without much excitement, then went into the kitchen for jelly doughnuts, to get the odd, tangy flesh taste out of our mouths. And then there was all that group activity back on the Army base I'd since tried not to think about. I'd been going into the woods to smoke cigarettes and pull down my pants with a gang of neighborhood misfits from another school for two years at Fort Rucker. Randy acted shocked when word reached him on the block that I'd been seen *butt-fucking* (actually a kind of non-insertive rutting) with Randall Tarp in an Off-Limits Zone. "You better not let Mom and Dad find out what you're up to," he warned darkly.

Although he was a little strange, dressing in an approximation of hippie garb (Army jacket and fringe vests) and carrying around fake joints he rolled from pencil shavings, compared to me Joey was a boy's boy. He cursed and spit, he could take apart his bike and put it back together; he had a chin-up bar in the doorway of the room he shared with two younger brothers, and noticeable biceps. It was like having the pet chimp I'd wanted ever since the TV show *The Hathaways* (which starred Peggy Cass as the mother of three chimpanzees): he swung from tree limbs and did handstands, he shouted nonsensical sounds when he was excited, and it seemed as if he just about always had a rigid erection jutting in his jeans. My mother said he was crude and complained that my room always stank after Joey had been over. It did; he carried around matches to light his farts.

In the back corner of the Carson's unlandscaped, broken-toy-, loose-brick-, and lumber-cluttered backyard, Joey had built a roofless two-by-four and plywood fort up on stilts, and that summer between seventh and eighth grade we slept there every Saturday and as many weeknights as my parents would permit. Sleeping out was thrilling: you were outside all night, directly under the disquieting black sky and stars, away from parental hearing and the childhood trappings of your own room, unprotected. I would anticipate one of these nights in Joey's fort all day, till I was almost sick with excitement. I might be reading one of my mother's book club Gothics in my frigid, air-conditioned room, or window-shopping at Bassett

Center with her, or mowing the lawn, but all the time I was thinking about what would happen that night.

Joey had recognized in me a fellow obsessive wanker; that was really what we had in common. I knew it deep down from the moment I stood on his erection. We were masturbating together in no time, squatting with our pants down in the blazing sun beside a dune on our desert forays, or lying on our dank sleeping bags up in the fort. At first we stared straight ahead; soon we were staring at each other's dicks and synchronizing our ejaculations.

We'd begin by playing cards or Monopoly by flashlight, stripped to our jockey shorts half inside our sleeping bags. Then we'd tell all the dirty jokes we knew, generally the same ones. We didn't laugh at the punch lines ("For a *nickel* I will!") after the first time, but raced ahead to the next. Then Joey would start talking about whatever girl he currently wanted to fuck. (At this time, it was Candy Reichstad, an older, hard-looking German exchange student with straight brown hair, to whom he'd never spoken a word. In fact, Candy dated GIs.) "I really got to shoot," he'd say. "Want to jack off?"

One night late in June we were winding up a marathon Monopoly game in the early hours of the morning. I was clearly losing; I almost always lost, too preoccupied with our near nakedness and Joey's warm breath in my face as we leaned across the tilting board to pay attention to the game.

"Let's say the loser has to do something. Whatever the winner tells him to do, he has to do it."

I nodded okay. I had a pretty good idea he wasn't going to ask me to steal a car.

Several rolls later I handed over my remaining pink and

yellow bills.

"You lose. Suck my dick."

"Uh-uh! I will not!" I knew I had to feign disgust. Strangely, I felt in control, as if I had plotted every step in our acquaintance up to precisely this event. "I'm not putting your dick in my mouth!"

"Look, you agreed the loser has to do what the winner says. C'mon. Hey, I'll do it to you too if you'll just do it first."

I didn't answer. He threw back his unzipped sleeping bag, a sweet odor of clean sweat and damp flannel and canvas wafting upward. We were both silent. A breeze was soughing through the willow trees surrounding the fort, and his chest tightened with goose bumps as he shivered once, his penis leaping whitely in the moonlight.

"C'mon—*please*, man."

I leaned toward him as he scooted further out of the bag, and took him in my hand. The excitement and guilt were dizzying. This wasn't like back in the woods when I was too little to reach orgasm, when I had no notion of *queer*, or consequences stronger than a spanking. I took the head of his dick in my mouth, shocked at the pure physical strangeness of it, certain I was making an irrevocable mistake (*Cocksucker!*), unbearably aroused. As he held my head and rocked in and out of my mouth, crooning, Joey was no longer the goofy, apish bike pal I thought I knew. Who I was now, I had no idea. My cowed, conforming self-image separated from me and rose into the night sky like the carefree ghosts leaving the wrecked roadster in *Topper*.

As we drove away from the officers' housing at Fort Rucker the year before, I'd imagined my experiments in the forest being dispersed around the globe with my Army-brat accomplices like the dismembered limbs of a corpse in a *True Detective* story. Now my underground life had reclaimed me. Nights up in the creaking fort, Joey and I dispensed with time-consuming board games and drew straws. I'd stolen a copy of *Teleny, or The Reverse of the Medal* from Randy's sock drawer, and we read aloud from its flowery descriptions of male couplings, and then ordered each other to act them out. I gritted my teeth when Joey slid inside me the first time, Wilde's purple commentary ("He pushed with all his might. The Rubicon was crossed!") before me.

Mornings, I'd wake feeling foul breathed and stained, unwilling to stay for pancakes flipped by Joey's excitable Seventh Day Adventist mom. He bounded up cheerfully; I couldn't wait to slink home and shower, brushing my teeth rigorously and gargling with Listerine. I'd avoid Joey for several days and cringe at his salacious monologues when we next went out riding. "*Hedda* likes you!" he'd shout over his shoulder, laughing. "Heada' my *dick!*"

With the return of my double life, I began to notice myself more critically in the mirror. Up till now I'd parted my hair on the side and trained my bangs across my forehead with HisSpray, believing implicitly my mother's assurance that I was a very handsome boy. Now the taunts of Dina Potter and her crew of furies rang true. I was an ugly, spotty fairy. I walked, ran, and threw like a girl. And I was pudgy. I had round cheeks and my mother bought me husky-size jeans. If I reached for the last cinnamon roll at breakfast, my older brother and father would turn and mouth, "Chipmunk cheeks!" Karl Brent's ordeals had shown that being overweight could push you over the line into public scapegoat and acknowledged queer, and I determined to shed my baby fat before September.

I accompanied my mother on her weekly visit to the commissary at Fort Bliss. As we glided down the air-conditioned aisles I looked skittishly away from the sunburnt and muscular young GIs and their teenage, pregnant wives pushing carts stacked with formula and disposable diapers, six-packs of Coors, and cartons of cigarettes and condoms. I scanned the shelves anxiously till I spotted them: box upon box of powdered Carnation Slender decorated with svelte women in swimsuits and laughing athletic men in tennis shorts. On the individual packets, a torrent of pink or brown or white liquid cascaded into a tall sundae glass. You drank it, and you became slim. I reached past the tired-looking, medicinal cans of Metrecal, which my father drank from time to time to no discernable effect, and selected several cartons of Chocolate Royale, Rich Vanilla, and Strawberry Supreme.

"Honey, you're going to starve! Just have one slice of pizza," my mom would say at dinner, shaking her head.

"I'll eat his share," said Randy, while I gurgled the chalky dregs of my Strawberry Supreme through a Dixie straw and sped out the back door.

"Why don't you just move in with Joey?" my father yelled.

I'd tell myself that each time with Joey would be the last, but soon enough I'd be locked in the bathroom feverishly masturbating as I replayed our last encounter or imagined things we might try next.

Like some Gothic secret that wouldn't stay bricked in, smirking references to homosexuality leapt out at me from magazine covers, my mother's latest Harold Robbins potboiler, and *The Tonight Show*. Every night Johnny would make a smug joke about Fire Island, in my mind a sort of *Gilligan's Island* where all the huts were well-appointed beauty parlors, since according to Johnny the place was jammed with nothing but hairdressers and decorators. Then Truman Capote would high-step out like a trained bear cub, slapping Johnny's hand coquettishly and baby-talking for fifteen minutes while I squirmed with embarrassment and my father fumed, "They ought to just shoot him."

The nights I didn't spend at Joey's, I often babysat for the young couples who ran around with my Aunt Janet and her husband. All the couples but Janet and Chris had new babies, and the work was easy, since most of the time the baby was already put down when I arrived and I spent the long evenings scanning trashy novels for sex scenes and masturbating with my face in a pair of Tip's or Dave's jockey shorts fished out of the hamper. The husbands were all good-looking, boyish jocks who made a point of offering me a Coors and leaving the latest *Playboy* on the coffee table. Then they'd have to drive me home at 2:00 A.M., drunk, flushed, and horny from flirting with each other's wives.

Tip, whose tow-headed infant Patsy screamed in my face for a solid hour before collapsing with her bottle while I sang her most of *The White Album*, was a hulking twenty-four-year-old baseball jock with big white teeth, a thick reddish-blond mustache, and massive arms heavily furred with platinum hair. Six years back he'd have been beating the shit out of me, but now he was roaring down the deserted interstate with me in his white Mustang, thighs spread wide, one hand on the bottom of the steering wheel, offering me a joint with the other.

"What are you now, thirteen? Shit, girls today, I bet you

get more pussy than me."

This was so ludicrously off-base I could make no answer, but that was okay. Like Joey, Tip liked to talk about sex. It was hell in that shithole 'Nam, he told me, but the hooch maids could give you a blowjob that felt like your brains were being yanked out the end of your dick. "Know what I mean?"

I knew. I glanced out of the corner of my eye at the bulge in his white jeans, and stared straight ahead.

"My you've gotten so slender," my mother said, without irony. "But honey, those bangs! You look like Veronica Lake!" She reached to smooth my hair back with a worried look. I'd starved myself slim over the summer, at the same time growing taller, and I'd fought and sulked to be allowed to keep my hair longer. We drove to the PX and Sears for new school clothes, and I chose tight, flared slacks, Day-Glo socks, and paisley shirts. The signature piece of my new look was a gold Nehru shirt worn with a glass-jeweled medallion on a large gold-colored chain. I thought I looked like Dickie Smothers, but my brother howled and said, "Whoa, *Sammy,* my main man!" Terry Blaine, a twice-flunked hood who'd spent time in the D-home for strong-arm robbery, pushed back his greasy hair and whistled as I walked briskly across the blacktop on the first day of school, my neck chafing against the stiff Nehru collar, medallion banging against my chest. "She's got a new figure!" he yelled after me.

"I think Brenda Smalley wants to go steady with me." I detailed the heady first few weeks of eighth grade in my diary with determined optimism. "Joey came up to me in the hall and said something dumb. He's so immature."

My homeroom teacher, Miss Boyd, liked me, and wrote

long, appreciative margin notes on the essays and stories I turned in. I was briefly celebrated for my vacation memoir, "The Dog Who Ate Beans," about a long family car trip to City of Rocks, New Mexico, with a flatulent dachshund, which was read aloud to all the eighth-grade English classes. This high profile backfired a week later when Miss Boyd read a Poe-inspired Gothic tale of mine to 8-C, and was interrupted by several of my PE persecutors shouting out, "He's a *fag!*" The class erupted in debate as to whether or not I truly was a fag, occasioning a tearful lecture on the cruelty of adolescents and a punitive homework assignment in the hated grammar text from Miss Boyd. Gwen Hindemuth, my steady of that week, reported all this to me at lunch, promising to stand by me through the scandal, and then breaking up with me by express note that afternoon—hardly living up to what had been our song, "Build Me Up Buttercup." My new persona was already wearing thin.

We had to dress out now for gym, and my head would ache from the strain of staring straight at my feet or into my locker while all around me, bumping and shoving in the narrow space between the waterlogged, sticky benches, sweaty boys yanked off torn blue gym shorts, and clenched, shocking, pale buttocks flashed dangerously at me from every direction. Bigger, more developed guys from the football team strutted around flipping their half-hard penises and smirking, waiting to catch you looking: *Whyn't you suck this for me?* Coach Brown, disturbingly attractive, with a lean, taut body and cold gray-blue eyes, sat in his glassed-in office, hairy legs up on his desk, scowling out at us, occasionally pretending to make some marks in a grade book. If you tried to rush through or skip the tense, crowded shower enclosure, he'd be up rapping at the window with his knuckles, yelling, "Bentley! You call that a shower? Get those panties off and get back in there before I come out and soap your pussy myself!"

The mumbled epithets I spent my days trying to avoid operated on one level, and had to do solely with bullying and the revenge of the stupid, who I could put in their place during the other six periods of the day. It was a practical, if formidable problem, trying not to get beat up or ostracized; it was a kind of dodgeball or hide-and-seek. My sense of injustice at being called a fag for hating sports was genuine. I went to dance parties in garages and backyards and went steady and broke up with girls. For the constant, hot undercurrent of desire that kept me terrified an erection might give me away in the rank proximity of the locker room, that drove me to my knees before the very worst of my oppressors in the secret hours of the night, I had no words.

I'd figured that the start of classes and fall weather would separate me from Joey. We didn't hang out together at school, and sleeping over was kid stuff. But two things happened that fall: my father was ordered to Germany for two years and we stayed behind, and Randy had a serious motorcycle accident and was in the military hospital across town for several months. My mother came home from teaching school to pick up my little brother and then rushed back out to visit Randy every night, leaving me alone in the house for hours. Joey would be at the door, or tapping at my bedroom window, moments after she backed out of the driveway.

We did it in the garage. One side was furnished with a rug, a TV set, and an old brown sectional couch from which strings of metallic thread hung like Christmas tinsel. We used the TV for light, reruns of *The Addams Family* and *The*

Munsters murmuring in the background, amid the odors of car exhaust and lawn mower. Sometimes we'd play strip poker and suck each other off. Often we improvised new scenarios. One of us might be stripped, blindfolded, and tied spread-eagled against the wall with ropes looped over the open rafters, while the other remained clothed, quietly detailing how we'd reached this moment, and what was going to happen next, dry mouthed and shaking with awe at our own imaginations. I might have to stand atop an old desk for ten minutes by the clock, bent over holding my ankles, while Joey inspected my ass, spreading the cheeks, slapping the backs of my legs with a ruler. Once he was a burglar armed with a toy pistol who broke in and made sexual demands at gunpoint.

Later, I'd be sitting on the orange-flowered couch in the den reading, legs still weak, my butt still sticky and throbbing, when my mother came home. "I worry about leaving you alone so much, sweetheart. Why don't you have one of your friends over?"

In January, Joey's father got a job offer in Dallas, and two weeks later, the Carson's house sat empty, a For Sale sign stuck in the weed-covered lawn. Just as suddenly as he'd dropped into my life, Joey was gone. I was stunned by my unforeseen reprieve; the steaming cracks in the earth closed up, and the ground trembled quietly. The following week I held hands with Fleur Patton at a party and asked her to go steady, but she declined in an enigmatic note.

One clear, cold March day I trudged up the short flight of steps from the subterranean locker room to the gravel school-yard, relieved as always to have made it through one more PE period relatively unscathed. We'd been playing basketball, and

while appearing to run after the ball wholeheartedly, I'd man-
aged to avoid contact with it completely, except for once
when someone slammed it into the back of my head. Down
in the changing area I'd pulled my clothes on without drying
off much and then stood at the sink a little longer than usual
getting my hair parted just right, a mistake. Anyone paying
too much attention to his hair or just standing in front of the
spotty mirror too long risked trouble. I knew I'd stepped over
the line when I caught Tommy Bradshaw's glance in the mirror as I combed my bangs across my forehead a second time
and he looked hurriedly away and spit noisily on the floor in
disgust. Tommy was one of those jocks who practically wept
if his team lost, and he despised me for sidestepping the ball
at crucial junctures, as if I were fumbling it on purpose. "You
could've had that one, asshole!" he'd shout at me. I knew
he'd jump at the chance to knock me down and kick me.

I was standing in the gravel outside the locker room
door when a hand snaked around the back of my head, fingers running roughly through my damp hair. "You sure got
your hair fixed real nice, Bentley. Makes me want to mess it
up." It was Bradshaw.

"Hey, cut it out, you're not funny!" My own words rang
mockingly back at me in a lispy, screechy fag voice. I was surrounded by jeering boys, somebody's arm around my neck in
a chokehold, lifting me off my feet. Hand after hand shot out
and ran through my hair; lips smacked inches from my face
with exaggerated kissing sounds. "Hey, he needs a hair treatment!" someone yelled, and then they were spitting on my
hair and rubbing it in. I lost my balance, tossed from one set
of gripping arms to another as if I were part of some improvised Martha Graham performance. All the fit, sinewy boys

I'd feared and craved encircled me, pawing, pinching, jab
bing, and roughly caressing my head, their faces, lips, leering
open mouths up close. I was turning dizzily, clinging to my
smart-boy dignity, *Cut it out!*—but the ground had split
open and the other me had spilled through. I wondered if I
would cry. My dick was hard. Terry Blaine's evil, beautiful
face shoved impossibly close, his lips almost touching mine.
He hawked and spit. "Fucking fag!"

The bell for fourth period rang. I picked myself up and
wiped the blood from my skinned palms on my pants, tucked
my ripped shirt back in, and walked into the biology lab,
climbing onto a stool next to my table mate, who pretended
not to notice my spittle covered hair all askew. I didn't go
home till lunchtime, and I didn't cry till I got there.

I didn't have sex with a man again till college.

The Satan Poster

...I lived in a world of dreams, drives, and desires...across which my conscious self desperately built its fragile bridges, for the childhood world within me was falling apart. —Hermann Hesse, *Demian*

Moving against the shuffling flow of other students, a stricken-looking teenager staggered down the glassed-in institutional hallway, peering among the crepe paper flowers, banners with peppy slogans, and construction paper goalposts of Homecoming Week in search of additional copies of the crudely Xeroxed poster, which, when spotted, she angrily snatched from the wall and added to the bundle of wadded-up paper in her other fist. I stood a few yards away staring into my open locker, my head aching from suppressed laughter. All morning I'd had to keep a straight face as I observed victims like Kitty Simpson, red-eyed with sobbing, shaking the curls of her blonde Farrah Fawcett mop in disbelief. Or tall, tidy Todd Armstrong, shrugging nervously and smoothing the air an inch away from his blown-dry hair with the palm of his hand as another letterman ambled over to ask if he'd seen it. Or Terry Siebert, leader of the Jesus freaks, nodding the renaissance halo of his red afro in solemn consultation with his disciples: Could this be the End Times? I swallowed a hiccup of laughter and leaned further into my locker. My fellow conspirators and I had avoided each other so far, afraid eye contact would release our stifled hilarity and give us away.

It had come about so spontaneously—that was the problem. One minute we were shooting the breeze in the journalism room after school on a dark fall evening of my senior year, and the next we were clipping photos and letters from old newspapers and yearbooks and arranging them on a blank piece of typing paper.

My first mistake was not realizing that everyone would simply assume I had done it.

My voice had still been childish in the little red pocket diary I kept in 1970, from the second half of eighth grade to the first semester of my freshman year at Greenvale High, in the El Paso housing subdivision of the same name, though it was neither green nor a valley. While I was avidly reading adult novels like *Myra Breckinridge, Portnoy's Complaint, The Fame Game,* and *The Crazy Ladies,* I was also, from January to August of that year, busily decorating the backyard clubhouse I'd cajoled my parents into buying me for my birthday. It was a cheap wooden playhouse bought across the border in Juarez; I at least had the sense to rip off the picket-fenced porch and shutters. I filled my diary entries with news of homework, the trials of PE, and a brisk baby-sitting schedule, signing off with a breezy *bye* or *see ya*. Three years later I was writing weekly "satires" for the school paper, driving a beat-up snot-green VW bug handed down from Randy, having sex with girls, and smoking pot and binge-drinking with a crew of fellow malcontents.

For the intervening period I remained the sort of pimply nobody you find if you glance through the tiny thumbnail photos of underclassmen interred in any old sour-smelling *Hoofbeats*, *Salute*, or *Bugler*. After Jocy conveniently moved away I had one companion, Robbie, a plump mama's boy I'd gotten to know in eighth grade because we were frequently seated beside each other alphabetically, or left among the undesired when teams were chosen for sports. At Greenvale he and I bought spirit ribbons, ate tasteless hamburgers on flour-dusted rolls in the snack bar, and snickered through the six-record performance of *Antigone* in Miss Penny's freshman English class. We joined Future Teachers of America and attended the Burning of the G. Every other week one of our mothers drove us to the dermatologist, who expressed our blackheads and pimples with a surgical tool and fed us tetracycline. During this time I fantasized and masturbated constantly about doing the things I'd done with Joey with various handsome and contemptuous boys I saw naked in PE, yet I still had no conscious conception of myself as homosexual and choosing to hide it. I expected that, unlike the dirty, guilt-ridden excitement my male fantasies gave me, sex with a girl would provide an emotional, soulful dimension that would supersede the other urge. I thought obsessively about the bodies of some of the brawny jocks or hairy hippie boys, but I didn't fall in love with them.

I still shared a bedroom with my eleven-year-old younger

brother and his spaghetti of bright orange Hot Wheels tracks. One early step away from that childhood world occurred not long after I received my driver's license at sixteen: I followed up on a card I found tucked into a copy of *The Fountainhead* at Bassett Center Bookstore (*Who Is John Galt?* read the provocative heading) and began attending Saturday night discussions with a gaggle of "Objectivists." This group of youngish singles looked nothing like their patron saint, a grim pixie in a black cape with a dollar-sign brooch whom I'd once seen on *The Tonight Show*. They met in the living rooms of those who didn't still live with their parents to listen reverently to a series of poor quality cassette recordings of Ayn Rand disciple Nathaniel Branden. They also drank a lot and had strictly rational affairs with each other, and being libertarians, they didn't think twice about serving bourbon and Cokes to a sixteen-year-old. I'd grow tipsy trying to focus on Branden's prissy Canadian twang ("Tonight we will be speaking of Objectivist epistemology…") while staring mesmerized at Fred, a dark-jawed, muscular engineer, who would be passionately making out with whichever female in the group he was currently dating. Not everybody would find the philosophy of Ayn Rand sexually exciting, but these people did.

Two significant changes took place in my junior year. I no longer had to take PE, and so was spared the daily bullying and fag-baiting during whatever ballgame Coach Conley, a skinny, bald redneck who resembled an unspooled mummy, ordered us to play, and denied the unsettling climate in the humid locker room beneath the concrete stadium. No more manning the clothes check baskets, as I'd been assigned to do most of sophomore year, alongside the lazily voluptuous Rick Chambers. When the others had jogged up the stairs and out to the blacktop for calisthenics and he and I were left to change last, he'd fondle his crotch and invite me to blow him. "C'mon, Bentley, why don't you just get down right here and suck it? You know you want to." But the jocks all talked to each other that way too. The correct response was, "You wish, you fag."

And that was also when I caught the attention of Delia Barton, Greenvale's journalism instructor and sponsor of the newspaper and yearbook, one of two outspoken women who oversaw the school's literary outlets. The other was Claire Meade, English teacher and sponsor of *Taps*, the literary magazine. Claire let me choose my own curriculum and write what I liked, and would eventually make me editor of the magazine. Delia, a thin, chic, high-strung woman with upswept silvery-blonde hair, held court perched upon a bank of several large business desks piled with typewriters, old newspapers, page proofs, contact sheets, type catalogs, and other thrilling journalistic paraphernalia.

Delia's teaching style was dramatic—she implored, wheedled, and threatened, waving her hands over her head, her fingers usually poised as if holding a cigarette or a piece of chalk, whether or not either one was there, gold bracelet jangling. She despised conformity, clichés, and most elected officials. The term *lady* was journalistic anathema to her: "We don't *know* if she's a lady!" She had a way of pronouncing the word *sweetie* with a degree of acid derision in the first sylla-ble that could reduce a Crockette—one of Greenvale's supra-cheerleader, high-kicking, pom-pom girls—to tears. Though she oversaw the chronicles of Greenvale's conformist elite, the *Cannon* and *Hoofbeats*, she loved her rebels best, and was most in her element hunkered down in the inner sanctum of her tiny back office lighting a Doral with a shaking hand, plotting strategy with whichever of her editors was about to be summoned to Principal Bosley's office over a controversial editorial, a suggestive headline, or, say, a caption beneath a photo of a dewy-eyed cheerleader watching a critical football game: *Anxious enthusiast contemplates big one.*

Every first-year journalism student had to turn in a complete mock-up issue of the *Cannon.* I took most of the task seriously, but, inspired by *The National Lampoon's* "Mrs. Agnew's Diary," a spoof of the Nixon administration, I made my column a dishy, first-person record of pious toadying, spying, and sniping—"Mrs. Livermore's Diary," based on a faculty member who set the standard for strict, dull, by-the-rules teaching. Like the fictional Mrs. Agnew, my Mrs. Livermore put a cluelessly perky but essentially mean-spirited spin on all she reported: she walked in on the principal bending the attendance lady over his desk and noted with satisfaction that the authorities were dealing more harshly with truancies. "I hear Mr. Bosley put a hair up Regina's ass over this, and I say high time!"

Ducky Livermore and her husband, Willard, attended Valley View Baptist Church, where my grandparents had belonged till they retired and moved to Abilene. Ducky was a pale, goody-two-shoes with prominent front teeth and goggly scared-horse eyes behind her thick-lensed, black cat-eye glasses. She wore penny loafers, frumpy plaid jumpers, and pleated, green-plaid skirts with a giant safety pin on the side. She was the antithesis of my pretty, twenty-six-year-old Aunt Janet, who taught world history at Greenvale. Janet's class was popular since she favored short skirts, showed lots of films, and staged history-themed *Jeopardy* tournaments. When Robbie and I went to see *Deliverance* at the Fox Cinema, we spotted Ducky and Willard several rows in front of us; just as Ned Beatty's baggy jockeys were being pawed off by the horny yokel about to sodomize him, Ducky ran awkwardly up the aisle, her husband close behind, but glancing back at the screen over his shoulder. I was impressed too—I could hardly tear my own gaze away from the scene, and I couldn't stop thinking about it till I'd gotten home, run a bath for cover, and masturbated twice, employing a Johnson's Shoe Polish dispenser as a dildo. Ned's pig squeals and the hillbilly's growls of "Gonna have us a *sow!*" instantly became part of the fag-baiting shorthand of the lettermen who preened like mermaids on a rock in the main hall between classes, combing their hair and flexing their muscles.

Delia read my project on a plane to Honolulu with her husband over Christmas break, upsetting a mai tai when she got to Ducky.

Upon her return I was appointed features editor, and began writing weekly spoofs: a parody of the student handbook or the new bell schedule; an exposé of a plot to smuggle classics into the library; an interview with the surprisingly subversive school mascot, "Wally," a stubby wooden crocodile in a cavalry uniform with a very phallic revolver poking out of his low-slung belt, who stood on his hind legs in the school lobby. A few months later I was named editor for the following year.

At about the same time, I got involved with Carlene, a tall, wild-haired, bookish girl in French class. Neither of us had really dated before. Initially antagonistic, we hissed insults at each other over the precious soundtrack to Madame Chumley's filmstrip of *Le Petit Prince*. As punishment for our classroom bickering, Madame Chumley teamed Carlene and me up for a project and the first evening we got together to work on it we conceived a stunt to shock everyone by pretending to have fallen in love. After a few staged dates and make-out sessions between classes, mock handholding turned to real.

Our relationship had peaked in intensity over the summer between junior and senior year—every evening we had sat necking in the dark on the cool cement slab in front of her family's typical faux hacienda tract house (the white gravel lawn punctuated with wobbly yucca and the ubiquitous orange-clay Mexicans snoozing with their sombrero-clad heads on their knees) or in my bedroom with Cat Stevens records turned up loud. My parents didn't like her (she tended to turn her head away, roll her eyes, and shriek with her peculiar staccato laughter whenever she met them), but they were visibly relieved to see me dating and only made vague suggestions that I not lock my bedroom door when I had company. At first I had enjoyed the baffled looks of the jocks and cheerleaders as we walked past them with our arms awkwardly laced around each other—the sissy and the shrew—but not a month into the new school year Carlene's shrill laugh was making me flinch, and I found myself preferring to hang out alone with my new friends from *Taps*, the *Cannon*, and *Hoofbeats*—Larry, a former jock; Emilio, a skinny Latino freak with an acid tongue and a cruel knack for mimicry; Alison, a long-red-haired yearbook staffer who'd thrown over her position as a Crockette and was nowadays heckled in the halls by the jocks she'd formerly accommodated as "B.J. Ali"; and Robbie, my faithful sidekick.

Larry had played football in junior high, but he had quit by the time we got to Greenvale. I well remembered him showing off a porn magazine he'd smuggled to school in a briefcase in the seventh grade, and posing around the sports field with his shirt off in eighth grade phys ed. Now, because of the newspaper, he'd become friendly with me. Sunday mornings he'd pick me up for the drive down I-10 to the Ochoa Brothers Printing Company, where we'd read galleys, cut copy, and add hot slugs of corrected type to the composed pages of the following week's *Cannon,* dizzied by the satisfyingly blue-collar fumes of oiled linotype presses and ink. Sometimes Delia chauffeured us in her huge beige Cadillac El Dorado with the Christmas tree air-freshener dangling from the rearview mirror and the sofa-like seats. Sometimes Larry came by for me in his father's car.

Larry, Alison, and I hung out after school working in the journalism room; other evenings we convened in Claire Meade's room, where Emilio and I reviewed submissions to *Tups;* soon we'd taken to partying in each other's bedrooms or, more often, in one of our cars, cruising out the highway or up and down quiet back roads, sipping can after can of Schlitz, or Seagrams 7 & 7s in plastic cups, and smoking pot.

That had first happened the previous spring: despite Delia's and Claire's best policing efforts, the annual journalism field trip to The University of Texas at Austin was a notorious debauch, and while I didn't get laid, I did get stoned, lying on a motel room bed with several grinning senior freaks, *Ziggy Stardust* blasting from a boom box. One evening soon after I got home Randy stuck his head in my room and plopped a fat lid down on my homework, just like the pusher in an after-school special.

Soshes, jocks, brains, dorks, Jesus freaks, and *freaks*—as non-conformers, hippies, and potheads were called, and referred to themselves; these were the cliques. I'd been invisible all my life, a dork at best. But now, passing joints between Emilio and Alison, or sucking down Schlitz with

The Satan Poster

Larry, I knew what I was: a freak.

Robbie had taken to debauchery as he had all my other interests, from repeated drive-in viewings of *Harold and Maude* and *Bananas* to the solo stylings of Mama Cass. Carlene, on the other hand, didn't mix well with my new friends. Her shrieks shattered the laid-back camaraderie of the dark backseat; I tired of trying to drink beer with one cramped arm always over her shoulders. Then I started going out without her, and before long I'd been casually seduced by the more experienced Alison, who had no intention of making me or anyone her boyfriend. My relations with girls seemed to increase Larry's desire to get me alone for beery heart-to-hearts. It was a running joke how many girls were desperately in love with him—but he had fallen in love with someone he couldn't have, and I listened sympathetically to his maundering about the pretty, vacuous Mala Parsons, a sophomore Crockette who flipped her straight blonde hair and ignored him.

Emilio's parents and sister were out of town, so Larry and I had come by to party at his house, a comfortable, run-down brick rancher in an older section of Greenvale, with wood paneling and blue shag carpet in the main rooms that always smelled of cigarettes and frying corn tortillas. I lay sprawled next to Larry on a sagging daybed, mouth pressed to a gurgling purple bong. We were watching a local Christian ministry channel. Women in gaudy ruffled outfits had been singing romantic ballads about being touched by Jesus; now the host was urging viewers with problems to call in for on-the-air healing. "Hey, should I?" Emilio asked, exhaling a stream of pot smoke.

"Yeah, do it!" I said, handing him the heavy, avocado-green phone. A moment later, we could see one of the bouffant-haired ladies in the tiered phone bank behind the host picking up.

"Um, yes, I've got a problem," Emilio whined into the receiver in a ludicrous, high-pitched, child's voice—a lot like the voice he used to imitate Carlene, actually. He waved us away with his free hand as Larry and I exploded with laughter, turning his back. Larry and I scrambled into the next room and fought over the pink princess phone there, cramming our heads together to listen in. "And what's your name, little girl?" asked the host, now on the line.

"*Ke*-vin."

"Bastard!" I yelled, hand over the receiver. Emilio was going on "...and my mother, she brings strange men home and then...and then she makes me..."

"*Your mother sucks cocks in Hell!*" I growled into the phone. There was a moment of stunned silence, and then we both slammed down the phone.

"You fucker!" Emilio shouted, rolling his bloodshot eyes and clutching at his long, wiry hair. "Are you crazy? You probably broke some Federal law and they're gonna trace the call to my house!"

"If little Kevin will just please call back—we seem to have lost our connection, and we know you need our help. Please call back—" Emilio snapped the TV off and we scrambled into our coats and ran, yelling and pushing, to the car.

I'd been frog-marched to Baptist church for sermons, revivals, Sunday school, and the cruelly misnamed Vacation Bible School for the first ten years of my life, and I resented and despised it. Greenvale's fundamentalist Christian parents were always storming to school to object to any hint of "humanism" or sex education. Carlene had been boning up for confirmation that summer; on several occasions I'd driven her to confession straight from an hour's necking and waited for her in the parking lot, the front of my jeans tented and wet, my fingers cramped and sticky. "Doesn't the priest get upset when you tell him about this?" I asked.

"Don't be silly, you don't talk about that kind of stuff!" she said impatiently, as if addressing an idiot, reapplying the pungent strawberry lip gloss she favored from a little pot.

These were the days of the Jesus People, when *Jesus Christ Superstar* was continually under production in one church basement or another, and faded-bell-bottomed, acne-spattered teens lugged their well-worn copies of *The Living Bible* with them to class. They prayed, or at least screwed their eyes shut and frowned in concentration frequently: in the mornings clutches of them huddled in the halls before the bell rang for first period, like the football team before a play (actually, the football team *did* pray in a standing circle before every game); during lunch break they sat holding hands in circles on the school lawn. They plastered the hallways with posters bearing Bible verses and news of the latest traveling tent revival or Jesus festival to be held at the Coliseum (a large El Paso auditorium; *Will there be lions?* I wanted to know). They looked at the rest of us with condescending pity, chatting excitedly with one another about the Rapture, that day when they would all disappear in the blink of an eye. *If only,* I thought.

I was lying on my bed reading one Saturday morning in late September when Emilio tapped at the window. His bulging eyes looked more crazed than usual behind his wire-rim specs. *"Jesus,* I've been up all night, man," he said when he'd come inside and flopped in a chair. "I had to finish that fucking book you gave me." I'd loaned him my copy of *Demian* a couple of days before. The night I finished it, I couldn't go to sleep when I turned out the light. My mind buzzing, I alternately wept and imagined showing up at Larry's house in the middle of the night and tapping on *his* window. So it didn't surprise me that the book could have this kind of effect on a person. It might as easily have been *A Separate Peace* or *The Bell Jar,* even *The Return of the Native,* with its malevolent fates and thwarted loves, had shaken me up for a week. It wasn't unusual for me to have my life changed by a book, or for me to sit through a movie like *Adam at Six A.M.,* starring Michael Douglas, or *Five Easy Pieces* twice in a row and then stay up all night on No-Doz, writing poems in the Rod McKuen/James Kavanaugh vein. But this was the first time I'd really seen Emilio anything but scathingly sarcastic—except for the Sunday a few weeks before when we'd taken a tiny chip of windowpane acid each and ridden out our hallucinations lying on our backs on boulders high up in the Ice Age rock formations of Hueco Tanks, just outside of town. Then, we'd been mostly silent and blissful. When we'd come down enough to drive back home late that afternoon, we were waylaid as we headed for my room and ended up sitting in the orange swivel dinette chairs in the kitchen, a Disney sunset flooding the room with golden light, while my mother—freshly lipsticked, her bouffant inflated from her weekly trip to the beauty parlor—glided around the room like Snow White with a songbird on her shoulder, serving up leftover chicken enchiladas. Emilio and I were both so overcome by the beauty of the day and the purity of the moment we had to wipe away tears. "You know I love you, right, Mom?" I said.

"Have you boys been drinking beer?" my mother trilled with raised eyebrows.

On this Saturday, we climbed into Emilio's rumbling, mufflerless Impala and smoked a joint as we drove to a derelict cemetery alongside I-10, where we wandered the kicked-over gravestones and mulled over *Demian* while Emilio snapped photos of me embracing wrecked sculptures, stretched out on overgrown plots, and finally, poking my head out of a giant urn.

One icy day in early October, Larry, Emilio, Alison, Carlene, Robbie, and I huddled beside Emilio's rusting maroon Impala in the parking lot pulling on the dingy black hooded cloaks we'd snitched from a storage closet in the drama department, left over from a production of *A Company of Wayward Saints*. I had typed up index cards with gibberish from Anton LaVey's *Satanic Bible* for us to chant; Emilio had stolen and thawed several chickens from his mother's freezer. I handed round the black candles and tried to light them with a shaking hand, but the matches kept going out, and the candles wouldn't stay lit in the cold breeze. It was the middle of first lunch break, and the prayer groups were eating their bag lunches, swapping conversion stories, and performing healings on each other in their usual two large circles either side of the main sidewalk on the front lawn.

"Okay, hoods up, heads down!" I said, and we threaded our way across the parking lot and up the sidewalk, waving our black candles and the bagged chickens we'd been too finicky to unwrap. I caught a glimpse of Alison's blue eyes and a strand of red hair falling out of her hood: she looked like Wendy the Good Little Witch in Harvey comics. I peered to one side: twenty bowed heads swiveled toward us as one. Several girls shrieked, as if their prayers had gone horribly wrong, and we picked up our pace, filing into the building, through the main hall, and out again, running across the blacktop to ditch our robes behind a portable classroom before they could rise and follow.

Jesus Festival posters had been peppering the school hallways since the previous year, similar in corny design to the Stamp Out Pot (STOP!) *Flower Power* posters, which depicted a muscular anthropomorphized flower flexing its biceps and grinding a joint underfoot. There were prayers at pep rallies and Campus Crusade for Christ hootenannies in the gym, and the growing prayer circles on the lawn. "What about separation of church and state?" I'd say to Emilio, Larry, or Alison, sitting around the journalism room typing up late copy or writing last-minute headlines long after school was out. "Yeah, it's an insult to atheists!" Larry said. Larry's Irish-Catholic father demanded that he attend mass as long as he still lived at home.

The poster seemed a logical next step. *Once-in-a-Lifetime Satan Festival,* the cutout ransom-note style letters read. In one upper corner, a madly smiling cheerleader gives *V*s for victory with both upraised hands: *Satan Saves!* At the bottom was a blurry group shot of one of the front lawn prayer circles captioned, *DEMONS—Harrowing testimonies of reclaimed souls from the ranks of the fearsome Jesus People!* Opposite that, the cutout head of a man in a clerical collar who looked a little like Principal Bosley: *Special appearance by our gracious Lucifer himself!* Dominating the poster was the clipped side view of

The Satan Poster

Kitty Simpson, wearing a puffed-sleeved pinafore, one arm extended, her hand sprinkling something into a plate, a look of expectant awe on her face. Tumbling upward in the crudely drawn flames that rose from her censer were class photos of five randomly chosen students who loosely represented groups we disdained: football star, Jesus freaks, a hippie guy who happened to look hilariously Satanic with his long black hair and Fu Manchu mustache, and Heidi Marona, a snippy fellow journalist and ambitious sosh. Seen in the context of the magic marker flames, the various phony smiles took on a significance that made us roll on the floor and laugh till our eyes watered and we gasped for air, as if possessed ourselves.

We had a hundred copies made at a print shop. Larry, Alison, and I let ourselves into the school late one weeknight with my journalism key, armed with Scotch tape and flashlights. Because the walls up and down the main hall were already jammed with Homecoming decorations, there was little chance a janitor would notice the posters and pull them down before morning. Humming the *Mission Impossible* theme, we moved quickly and were out of the building and driving down Carlsbad Highway with a lit joint and cold beers in twenty minutes.

Most of them were ripped down before noon, but the reaction kept building beyond anything we'd imagined. People discussed it excitedly all day long; that night, Emilio, Larry, Alison, Carlene, and I called each other to trade stories. "I heard two girls in the bathroom saying there's a coven of witches that did it," Alison said, giggling nervously. I could hear her mother, the organist at her Presbyterian church, conducting a piano lesson in the background. Word was, Kitty

Simpson's pastor had been seen going into Mr. Bosley's office. The next day, Delia and Claire cornered me in the journalism office and shut the door. "Bill Bosley's positive you did it," Claire said. "It's so sloppy—it's not even funny. If you did it, it would be properly punctuated, right? Look me in the eye and tell me you didn't do it, Bentley." Her indignant, forthright country voice, clear blue eyes, and solid body in her blue-striped dress were everything right and good.

"I didn't do it," I said evenly. Wouldn't this thing just blow over?

Delia stubbed out a half-smoked Doral and lit another. "*Look*, Bentley, Bosley says it's up to us to prove you didn't do this. We've been swearing up and down you'd never do something so stupid."

They went out sleuthing with a copy of the poster and the previous year's yearbook, the theme of which had been *Things Worthwhile*, methodically visiting local copy shops; the second guy they talked to, the elderly Mexican owner of Tico's Copy House, pointed to my junior class photo. "That's the one—but hair much longer, and he got little mustache," he said, fingering his own. They drove out the highway and parked for an hour in the desert, passing a bottle of vodka back and forth and crying.

Claire called me later that night. "We know you did it, you little bastard. I suppose your friends helped you?" I remained silent. "We have to tell Bosley. Tell me, why Heidi Marona?" Heidi's mother also taught at Greenvale, and was pals with Claire and Delia. Alison and Carlene had both insisted on Heidi. She was, as my grandmother liked to say, a bitch from way back. And her crude attempts at hipness or popularity, which always rang false, embarrassed me. What was it

The Satan Poster

Pistorius told Sinclair in *Demian?* I flipped back through the book to find the lines: *The person whom you would like to do away with is of course never Mr. X but merely a disguise. If you hate a person, you hate something in him that is part of yourself. What isn't part of ourselves doesn't disturb us.*

He let me squirm till third period, then, as I sat listening to Mrs. Meade reading aloud from Steinbeck's "Flight," a story about a Mexican boy fleeing the law up a rugged mountain (I loved the soothing inflections of her voice and the way her honest Texas accent pronounced the fugitive protagonist's name *Pay-pay*), the squawk box sizzled and Mr. Bosley called me to his office.

He was situated in a front corner of the building with large windows from which he could survey the parking lot and lawns. There was wood paneling, a glass case full of athletic trophies, and several primary-colored casual chairs opposite his large, uncluttered desk with its plastic *World's Greatest Principal* statuette beside a framed family photo. The last time I'd been there my photo was being taken receiving a plaque for winning the Hudspeth County Soil and Water Conservation prize for my entry in the "Our Soil—Our Strength!" essay contest. Bill Bosley was, like most El Paso District principals, a former coach, proficient in push-ups and discipline. He was a humorless man with a piercing blue evangelical stare, who'd been pissed off ever since he'd lost the power to send boys home for having hair over their collars or untucked shirts.

"I wish you would just explain to me why an intelligent young man like you would do something like this." I wasn't going to get anywhere arguing about the propriety of religious activities on campus with this wild-eyed Baptist. "It was just a joke that got out of hand." Like when a couple of drunken lettermen kidnapped Wally and left him posed as if attempting to make a sow of Big Boy, the checkered-overalled icon in front of Shoney's Big Boy Burger, I thought.

He studied a formerly crumpled copy of the poster for a moment. "I feel sorry for anyone with such a warped sense of humor he thinks this is funny." It appeared I was going to be eating some of the soil I'd praised. "You know, you're obviously a talented young man, but the trouble with you is, you're *bent in the wrong direction.*"

There was an awkward silence during which I waited without much hope to see if he was going to laugh at his little pun. "Well. You're suspended for two days. Get your things and go home. And tuck in that shirt."

It was decided that I would lose the editorship of the paper, but remain editor of the literary magazine, *Taps*, as it didn't come out till May, by which time the scandal should have abated. Letting the punishment fit the crime, Delia made Heidi Marona editor of the *Cannon*. The two-day suspension actually provided me with a convenient lying-low period, as it had been put about that certain outraged jocks were threatening to teach me a more physical lesson. But I would have to apologize, in person, to Kitty Simpson's parents.

"Why? Why our daughter? Why make Kitty the high priestess? You know, everybody thinks because she's beautiful and popular everything's been easy for Kitty, but she's just as insecure and sensitive as anyone else!" I didn't point out that we'd clipped Kitty's picture on a whim, mainly because a yearbook photo of her at the traditional Burning of the *G* showed her posed in a way that made it easy for Emilio to draw the flaming censer in her hands. If we'd meant to persecute someone beautiful and popular, there were plenty of more qualified candidates.

"That's right, Mother. I have feelings too!" Kitty's chapped lower lip trembled. Though I didn't dare look, I felt Carlene's shoulder next to me shaking: either she was sobbing or about to laugh. Why had I agreed to let her come in with me?

"Well, I just want to say how sorry I am that we hurt Kitty's feelings," I said soberly. I was sorry I was sitting here now, groveling, on a pink-flowered couch in the Simpson's salmon-colored living room, that much was true.

"He's lying, Daddy," Kitty said. If she wasn't Satan's High Priestess, she was well on her way, I thought. "He's not really sorry. Oh, why do they hate me so?" Kitty wailed, and burst into tears.

"That's enough, Kitty," said Mr. Simpson. "I want you to know we thought of talking to a lawyer, young man." Carlene began to sob beside me. Was it real? I had no idea.

"...so *very* sorry. We just didn't think about what we were doing." I felt like a hideous ventriloquist's dummy; I hardly knew what was coming out of my mouth.

I still felt that way several hours later as I caddishly used the crisis atmosphere to finalize my breakup with Carlene. We sat parked in her driveway in the cold, dark pod of my ramshackle Volkswagon. "I don't *understand!* Are you saying you don't want to *see* me anymore?" She began to keen, her mouth hanging open, her nose running unchecked.

"I just don't want to be a couple anymore. We'll still be

friends..." She scrambled to find the door handle in the dark, half tumbled, half jumped from the car, and ran into the house, probably to draft the first of a string of rather good Anne Sexton-style poems she'd submit to *Taps*, about a fragile girl whose heart is broken by a cruel oaf.

Streaking was Larry's idea. "Are you crazy?" Emilio laughed. "Isn't that what your fag jock friends do?" A letterman had streaked the pep rally the week before—flashed, really; he ran naked between parked cars beyond the football field and only a few people actually saw him. I'd gone straight from Carlene's to Larry's; we'd picked up Robbie, Emilio (who took the wheel so I could climb in back with Larry), and several six-packs.

"C'mon Kevin, let's show these pussies how it's done," Larry said, grabbing my shoulder. "Emilio, wait for us on the other side." Even as I laughed at the ridiculousness of it I knew I was going to do it. Larry had already kicked off his loafers and was yanking his bulky sweater and T-shirt over his head. The close enclosure of the VW blossomed with the funky odors of shoes, socks, and wet armpits. "Hurry up, man! It's fuckin' freezing!" I fought my way out of my clothes and followed the white of Larry's fleshy ass and broad shoulders, catching a glimpse of swinging scrotum between his legs as he climbed out of the car ahead of me. The big flat park was pitch dark except for the glow of lighting around the small children's playground in the middle with the giant monkey-bar rocket and slide. It was past midnight on a school night; the park was deserted, the street dead. "Once around the playground, then the rest of the way across the park," he breathed into my ear, and then we both took off running, shouting and wincing when our bare feet hit rocks or stickers. He reached the playground before me and cantered playfully around it, then, whooping, leapt at the crossbar of a swing set and executed a series of pull-ups and flips. The jolting sight of his naked body, white under the big lights—the dark patches of his pubic hair and armpits, his cold-shrunken dick and balls—brought me to a halt. I stood, arms crossed, shivering, so overwhelmed by his nakedness I forgot my own, looking at him, the first naked boy I'd dared to look directly at since Joey; the boy, I realized, I loved.

The horn bleated in the distance, and then the strains of Bowie's "Drive-In Saturday" pouring from the radio rose in volume as I turned to see the VW lumbering up the curb, onto the grass, and toward us. "Get in, you idiots!" Emilio yelled. "I don't believe this!"

Several hours later, half passed out, half feigning to be, I was carried into my dark house between Larry and Emilio. "He shouldn't have had that last beer; he's a real lightweight," Larry stage-whispered to Emilio, whose impatient shrug I could sense. The concern in Larry's voice made my eyes well up in the dark. Somebody pulled back the bedclothes; Larry wrestled off my shoes, shirt, and jeans, and flipped the covers over me. Then they left, stumbling, belching, and bumping the furniture.

Servo-Robots
in Bondage

I was crouching on the freshly mown grass at Stone Knoll, my long, feathery hair still damp from the shower, wearing a touch of my mother's green eye shadow I'd sampled on my way out of the house and a puka shell choker around my neck—which was appropriate, as I was on my way to Geology. I'd just sat cross-legged and smoked a quick couple of pipes with William and Wayne before they departed for the art and drama departments respectively; now I was deciding if I wasn't too stoned to identify rocks, or whether I'd cut class and hang out.

"Oh... Kevin, how's it going?" I looked up into the glare to make out the handsome, depressed-looking features of my one-time crush, Larry. Larry still got haircuts, took school seriously, and only partied on the weekends, though I noticed he was wearing a tight, black-and-gold tiger-striped shirt of some shiny, man-made material, open to mid-chest.

We'd stopped doing things together soon after graduation.

"Pretty good. Keeping busy."

"Yeah? I heard you're hanging out with Wayne Connor. I thought he joined the Army."

"He's out now. Yeah, you know, I'm just running around with him and William, and, you know, Emilio and Robbie."

"You seeing anyone?"

"Not really." I was seeing Wayne, as far as I was concerned.

"Nice necklace."

"Nice clogs."

"Fuck you. Listen man, I gotta get to class. Let's get together sometime, all right?"

"Yeah, definitely. Later." That had been awkward. We were never going to get together. I was a stoner and, though I hadn't exactly come out, to myself or the world, the word was already out that I was a fag. Certainly anyone with the patience to wade through one of the obtuse poems I was submitting to the campus lit mag, *Headframe,* now edited by my friend Emilio, knew. After my Bowie-inspired lines about late-night sex in the desert, "Android Epithalamion," appeared, my friend Gerald parodied it in the following issue: *Servo-robots in bondage/Servo-robots in ecstasy/Don't sit next to me/Or cathect with me/When you intersect with me...* There was no mistaking the words *glittering and gay/in our bold butane brassieres.*

If I skipped class and waited over by the fountain in front of Badley Hall, I could catch Wayne coming out and see if he wanted to have lunch together, or maybe just go smoke a joint in one of the network of drainage tunnels around campus that served as pot-smoking dens. The university's dated Tibetan architecture, which resembled a down-at-heel Shangri-la, perched on hills overlooking the squalid cardboard huts of Juarez—referred to lightheartedly as Bedrock—just across the brackish Rio Grande. I got up and walked toward a beige stucco monolith.

Wayne Connor was an Olympian senior I'd admired from afar as an unformed sophomore in high school. Wayne, the handsome, rebellious writer and student council president, surprised everyone by following his practical-minded girlfriend into the Army after graduation. He was discharged and back in El Paso by the time I graduated two years later, Corporal Shelly having dumped him for an officer. He was tall, pale, and naturally muscular (he'd quit the basketball team rather than cut his hair) and I'd long fantasized about knowing him, being his best friend, and talking about our writing together. I pictured us as James Dean and Sal Mineo; but in *my* movie, Natalie would have an earlier curfew.

We first actually met at a small gathering of former creative writing students at Claire Meade's house on a warm summer night shortly after graduation. His lank blond hair hadn't yet grown out of the Army buzz cut, which emphasized his broad forehead and large, excited, myopic blue eyes. "If you aren't two of a kind!" Claire laughed, shaking her head with feigned disapproval at some anarchistic wisecrack. Our school careers had been strikingly similar: academic honors marred by censorship showdowns with Principal Bosley. This was not entirely a coincidence, since on some level I'd modeled myself after Wayne. Unaware of my Eve Harrington potential, after several hours' conversation and three beers,

he seemed flattered and smitten. What for me had been a distant case of hero worship, quickly escalated to feverish infat-
uation. By the end of the evening I'd offered him a ride
home and he and I were speeding down I-10 in my faded
green '62 Bug, sharing a joint and tales of disillusion over our
ex-girlfriends.

Within a week of our meeting at Claire's, Wayne and his
sidekick, William, formerly Greenvale High's most notorious
freak (he once painted an American flag on his face and
walked to school barefoot in the snow, carrying a lily) had
merged with my remaining dope buddies, Robbie and
Emilio. We'd hang together for hours in William's junk-
crammed room at the top of a derelict split-level known as
Ha! Ha! House because of the laughing Mr. Natural silhou-
ette he'd taped to his window, flummoxing the suburban
Catholic Church congregation across the street. A priest
came to the door to complain about it, and William's mother,
Frieda, a ditzy Christian Scientist, invited him in for Kool-
Aid and Hydrox cookies, but couldn't see his point.

Frieda had stopped climbing the cluttered stairs to
William's room several years back; instead she stacked clean
laundry on the bottom step and shouted up when someone
came over or called. When we'd all piled up the stairs and
into his musty room, William would shut his door, gesture
guests toward piles of clothes and old barstools, and start
handing around bongs. You exhaled deeply, then sucked at
one end of a two-foot purple plastic cylinder while he held
out a match; when the ashes shot through the bowl you fell
back with a pale face and bursting lungs, head reeling and
ears buzzing. Then, in a few quick seconds, time seemed to
arch its back and stretch; the light in the room grew achingly

sharp and clear yet viscous, subterranean, as if we'd all gone to the bottom of the ocean together in a diving bell.

With his delicate face and long uncombed brown hair, ragtag military surplus, and printmaking ink scoring his arms like tattoos, William might have stepped out of a road show production of *Oliver!* He spoke sparingly in a cranky, falsetto voice, which was eerie and charming, though you had to wonder if he didn't actually have a regular voice that he just wasn't using.

My excitement over getting to know Wayne cast the whole group in a kind of amber glow during that long, dreamlike summer and fall of '74. We went on bike rides, hikes, and ill equipped camping trips during which we took acid so strong it loosened our fillings and pinned us laughing and weeping to the spinning planet, to a bleary soundtrack of Genesis, Yes, and Pink Floyd.

Often when I was out driving around smoking dope with Wayne and the others that fall, against my father's express orders I'd steer my beat-up Bug off the highway and into the desert to play bumper car, swerving down circling dirt roads, spinning the wheel and caroming harmlessly off surrounding dunes, the car rank with pot smoke. One night I schemed my way to taking one of these desert jaunts alone with Wayne.

The car thumped into a dune and I switched off the engine, leaving us in silence and moonlight. We leaned back in our seats, knees on the dashboard, chatting comfortably and passing a fat joint back and forth. When I asked for a shotgun—as we all regularly did, scrupulously acting as if there was nothing significant about putting your lips a few inches from another guy's and blowing smoke down his throat—Wayne complied without missing a beat. He was sadly retelling some anecdote of happier days with Shelly Marshall when I took advantage of a musing pause to throw my arm chummily over his shoulder.

"What would you think if I said I loved you?" I asked, staring out the windshield.

"*Whew!*" he said, whipping his head around in one of his trademark cartoonish doubletakes, as if Road Runner had just shot by. Then, more slowly: "I'd say I really like you a lot too." His door was jammed against a bank of tumbleweed. I could see the whites of his large eyes in the bright moonlight as he weighed his predicament. I was gambling everything, but I knew I couldn't go another day without declaring my love. He might laugh in my face, he might never talk to me again, but just saying it, telling him, made it real.

"*No*, I mean I *love* you. I've been in love with you since the first time I saw you. I loved you when you pushed away Bosley's hand instead of shaking it at graduation." I let one tear roll down my cheek, and saw that he saw it. He made a tender sound, half concern, half desperation.

"This same thing happened to me with my best friend in the Army," he said, shaking his head, "and that didn't exactly work out. I just don't think I'm gay, see?"

"Me either," I said, carefully—though I was feeling more certain every second. I leaned into his face to kiss him then, and when he turned away a fraction and I followed, he gave in, and then the beauty of it was I was kissing him, I was kissing Wayne Connor—and however reluctantly, he was opening his lips and letting me, sighing as his tongue rolled out of hiding and poked into my mouth. As we embraced the windows fogged up and, along with the haze of marijuana, the air began to reek of perspiration and Herbal Essence shampoo. I scrambled over the long gear shift, my jeans half down, to press myself against him, stroking his head, sniffing the small, damp patch of pale hair in the center of his chest, sucking on his full lower lip. In spite of his being older and physically bigger, Wayne's ambivalence made me feel I was ravishing him, and I didn't pause to ask before wrestling his straining penis out of his pants.

"I'm not sure I can do this," he said. "Actually, I haven't come since Shelly..." I had slipped down for a closer look; his sturdy erection thumped my face. I took him in my mouth, grabbing his hand and putting it on my dick. I hadn't had sex with a guy since Joey had moved away and I'd sworn off at thirteen, but my actions seemed familiar and inevitable as marching down the aisle at graduation.

After an hour's efforts—after I'd twice noisily ejaculated onto his pants leg and shoes—I was willing to concede defeat, for now. His dick was big, it was hard, but it was looking dangerously chafed and it wasn't going to shoot.

"You aren't the first to try," Wayne said woefully, jamming the stubborn monster back into his Levi's. "I just haven't been able to have an orgasm since Shelly and I broke up."

Wayne tried to avoid being alone with me after this, but I was usually the one driving and I made a point of dropping him off last. When he couldn't politely escape them, he suffered my assaults with abashment and a kind of detached cooperation that is difficult, thirty years later, to fathom. But in all my attempts at making love with Wayne, he fell well short of passion. He was like one of those Dancing Tilly dolls all the girls on my block had when I was small. They were life-size, slack, gamely smiling rag dolls whose feet you'd strap to yours and then go waltzing off, but you always knew it was you doing the dancing.

One Saturday night Wayne and I took our mothers to a local theater production of *Forty Carats*. In my addled mind it was a date. Earlier that day, I'd presented him with a silver-plated cigarette case I'd cashed in my childhood coin collection to buy. Both our moms were grade school teachers; both, until recently, had been proud of their brainy, witty sons. The conversation at intermission was awkward. Mrs. Connor was a fairly hip divorcée and an object of alarm to my self-effacing mother, who liked to keep a low profile and never risked incurring anyone's disapproval.

Wayne's hair had reached Fab Four length; mine hit my shoulders. I had picked up a lot of new gestures that involved flipping it back or sweeping it out of my eyes. My father would cringe and mutter, but he'd already had to face my guitar-playing older brother Randy's long and aggressively disarrayed hair, so mine didn't immediately announce my aberrant sexuality. I had noticed him eyeing me suspiciously a couple of times as I gushed about Wayne or William over one of my mother's cream-of-mushroom-soup casseroles at the dinner table, tossing my hair like Peggy Lipton.

Mrs. Connor had sized me up fast and didn't like what she saw. Wayne, I'd slowly begun to learn, was a *fauxmosexual:* he didn't seem to be interested in girls (other than the much-lamented Shelly) and he was extremely close to his mom, confiding everything. So I had good reason to tremble when she fixed me with her heavily mascaraed eyes and sweetly smiled. We were all standing in the mildewy basement lobby of the Upstairs Downstairs Theater, holding Dixie cups of Chablis (except for my mother, who sipped a Diet Coke). "Honey, you have the finest hair," Mrs. Connor said, reaching out to touch it, her bracelets jangling. "It's a shame you're not a girl. You know, you ought to part it on the side—it'd be much prettier."

Between semesters we pooled our savings—Wayne, William, Emilio, Robbie, and me—and Wayne's GI Bill checks, and rented a townhouse in a complex alongside campus, the Waymore. *Waymore drugs*, we said. We moved in on New Year's Eve. Emilio borrowed an old flatbed truck from an uncle and drove it by each of our houses to load up. William brought a stuffed laundry bag and a psychedelically painted mannequin, Wayne just a duffel bag; Emilio carted along his darkroom equipment. They would all crash in sleeping bags in rooms divided by hanging sheets, William's decorated with dozens of his latest printmaking efforts (I was particularly thrilled by one depicting a naked figure, recognizably me, running toward a boiling green and orange sunset). Robbie and I moved our entire bedrooms, which furnished the room we shared as well as the living room, down to my desk, stereo, and Pier 1 beaded curtain.

When we'd lugged everything in, unpacked, and begun passing bongs, lolling around the living room floor on cushions, *Nursery Cryme* wafting from the stereo, my beads swaying and clacking in the doorway, it seemed life had reached its apex. "Well, isn't *this* cozy?" William drawled in his scratchy, Mighty Mouse voice after a stoned lull in the conversation, exhaling a bongful of pot smoke, and we all screamed with laughter and collapsed in coughing fits. Wayne stood up and shook his hair like a wet dog. "I'm going to see what's happening at that drama department party," he said, pulling on his ripped jean jacket and walking out.

Contrary to what I'd expected, now that we were all living together, it was easier for Wayne to escape being alone with me. I'd begun to see him differently anyway, my exaggerated admiration souring. How could someone who appeared so masculine be such a fussy old maid? It grated on me when he'd glance nervously around for a clock, asking querulously, "I *wonder* what time it's gotten to be?" When we'd all sat in a circle on the shag carpet smoking bongs for an hour, he'd suddenly clutch his hair, roll his eyes and moan, "Oh my! How did I ever get so stoned?" as if that wasn't to be expected by now, or as if he'd been dragged there and forced to inhale. I sneered as I watched him tip back his big baby-face to plop Visine into his red eyes. At moments it seemed my frustrated passion had transformed me from a mopey, Phil Collins-humming love-sot to a sharp-tongued queen.

Back when we were planning the move, Robbie, Emilio, and I had said we'd get part-time jobs, but none of us ever did. We lived on our allowances and gas money and Wayne paid the rent. Like any college dorm, the apartment was for partying, crashing, and occasionally studying. We rarely used the kitchen, gorging on flying visits home and smuggling food back. I did most of my reading and writing over endless cups of coffee at Sambo's and Denny's.

Before the Waymore we'd done varying strengths of LSD together on several occasions: purple microdot, blue cheer, blotter (tiny tabs of paper stamped with the winsome images of Mr. Natural or Mickey Mouse). We'd always taken acid at carefully chosen natural locations, with a planned peaceful and pleasant agenda to insure good trips. Now Gerald, who still lived at home, suggested he discreetly store his huge acid stash at our place, in payment for which we could have all we wanted at bulk rate. Gerald was an odd duck I'd known since the eighth grade; he used to wander around the playground in

plaid slacks and horizontally striped T-shirts reciting adver-
tisements for imaginary products like "Corn Wimpies." When
we were freshmen he conceived and wrote the scenario for my
first eight-millimeter film, *Dwellers of the Black Commode,*
which began, "Anus Dolt reached in vain for the remaining
square of tissue on the empty roll as he swirled down, down,
down in a fetid sea of bright blue and dark brown...." Gerald
had a habit of fixing on some arcane or obscene catch phrase
and then repeating it till he drove everyone around him
mad—"Rip off her drawers and get a little!" from a Frank
Zappa ditty was a favorite—much the same way my grandfather seized on advertising jingles that struck his fancy, repeating them as if making a judicious statement in all situations.
"Grandpa, I've shut your finger in the car door!" I might say.
"That's what I said, Mead's Fine Bread," he'd reply, with nary
a grimace. Later he opted for "'Atsa some spicy meatball,"
which saw him to the grave.

Thanks to Gerald, in short order we had organized our
lives around a three-inch Sucrets tin full of miniscule tabs of
amber-colored Windowpane, like obliging lab rats, tripping
pretty much every day, or night. The idea was to take it and
then not talk about it—to "maintain." Why was it appealing
to render myself half-psychotic and head out for some simple
activity, handicapped with sandbags and blinders like a character from Vonnegut's "Harrison Bergeron"? I wanted to be
blasted out of my humdrum West Texas world, and I still
longed to be intimate with Wayne and, more and more,
William; for a brief time, tripping seemed to accomplish these
things. In the emotionally raw state of tripping, which ren-
dered the most mundane sight, thought, or action monu-
mentally weird, charged, and holy, loving men and having sex

with them was no stranger than anything else.

We'd emerge from a movie theater wildly hallucinating, quivering from the effort of crossing the street on a green light. "Let's take a walk in the desert!" someone would say, and off we'd go, woodenly staggering over cacti, tarantulas, and lizards. "Wow, look at the moon!" we'd shout with simple delight. "Man, doesn't that shadow look like a giant Nazi?" Eventually we'd come down sufficiently to scatter to our mattresses in different corners of the apartment, where we'd vibrate and grind our teeth.

Now and then I'd manage to get William's sole attention—hiking together in the desert or camping in nearby New Mexico's Organ Mountains. Then I loved him best, with his odd fascinations, creaky voice, and paint-scarred, beautiful face. Shortly after the move we'd begun having sporadic sex, always silent and unacknowledged. After an evening of tripping William might come crawling into my bed, blue poster paint coating his skin, or a sheep's pelvis bone rubber-banded onto his head like some creature out of H. P. Lovecraft. Hallucinating, I couldn't tell where my body ended and his began. That he could violently pin me down and penetrate me one minute, and lie passively while I shoved my cock into him the next seemed bound up in this purifying loss of a clearly delineated identity I experienced on acid.

William and Wayne had been friends since high school and there seemed to be a tacit understanding that William would always be taken care of. Were they lovers? I wondered jealously—no, but William clearly loved Wayne, and Wayne seemed to aspire to know and emulate William, as I had Wayne.

Though he kept a sleeping bag in a corner and, like

William, dragged home weird objects he found in the desert or on the street for art projects, or sometimes spent hours in the darkroom he'd made of the downstairs bathroom, Emilio spent the least time of any of us actually in the apartment. He was wary but cool about what he saw going on between me and the two older boys; he worked with a gay guy at the lit mag. "They seem to be coming out of the woodwork," he said.

I was just able to keep up with the heavy reading required for my lit courses, but my social skills were deteriorating. Wayne and I shared a writing class, giggling rudely at readings by certain other students, for whom we invented names like Eggnog von Overture, Groovy Girl, and The Borax Twins. My nemesis was a perky elderly lady who favored hats festooned with plastic flowers and performed frequent dramatic recitations of her irksome verse, which usually began with a daisy on a sunshiny day and ended up with the smiling Savior nodding on his cross.

One day I read aloud a story of my own about a workshop monopolized by a simple-minded, attention-grabbing old woman, "Burying Hilda." Dr. Raddison might have been willing to laugh at Edwina, but it was foolhardy of me to also lampoon his tedious readings from his own hard-boiled detective fiction—and his difficulty with *R*s. My screed met with stunned silence and hostile stares. After I cut the next class, Wayne, who'd gone, suggested that I might want to consider dropping. "Man, you really made those people hate you," he said, looking at me thoughtfully.

And you made me do it, I told myself.

By now I wasn't the only guy with a frustrated crush on Wayne. Among his new friends from the drama department, mostly fauxmosexuals, was one real McCoy: Art Zelinksky. Art had become Wayne's inseparable companion after they'd been paired in several improvisations and one acts. Art was the first loudly out homosexual I'd ever met, and the prospect was worrying. Short, wiry, and sallow, with hideous acne scars, tobacco-stained yellow teeth, and a permed 'fro, he lisped, screamed, and snarled, keeping up a constant barrage of scathing insults, mimicry and innuendo. He addressed the butchest jocks as "girl," and performed vicious impressions of the department's star actress, a bony blonde who talked through her nose. Of course he recognized me as a fellow traveler instantly, and my jealousy. "I've been out all day with your boyfriend again! Don't worry, her virtue's intact," he'd bray, swaggering into the apartment with Wayne, who, like everyone, laughed helplessly at Art's quips and ignored his insults and sexual suggestions. "How's everything here at Miss Labia's School for Girls?" Was this what being gay would mean? What if this was how people already saw me?

Waymore *unbearable*, more like. There was always a circle of people sitting or lying on the floor in the living room getting stoned. It was hard to declare a homework night for myself and then try to read Milton while people with glitter and Day-Glo paint on their faces shrieked up and down the stairs and slung the squares of mirrored glass William stockpiled off the balcony to shatter on the desert rocks below.

I found myself sulky and resentful most of the time now, and in no state of mind for dewy-eyed tripping. Still, I'd melt a chip of the bitter, gnat-tasting Windowpane on my tongue and head out with the others on the regular midnight hikes to watch the molten ore pour from a massive mechanical bucket at a nearby smelting plant. Once I got high, though,

I couldn't think of anything but my disappointment that Wayne, and now William, had failed to fall in love with me. In a landscape out of *Paradise Lost*, I ground my teeth and thought of Satan's misery as I stared at the flowing ore and breathed the odors of sulfur and, strangely, frying bacon: *Which way I fly is Hell; myself am Hell....*

One afternoon I sat in on Wayne's drama class to watch the scene he'd been rehearsing with Art, the climactic, cruel phone game from *The Boys in the Band*. To show range, Wayne was playing gay Michael and Art was Alan, the straight college chum. Wayne's Michael was understated and touching; Art's Alan was a camp classic of nervous masculinity. He was, I saw clearly, impersonating Wayne. I walked out while they were still wrestling over the phone, before Alan could dial Fran.

Emilio was the first to crack. When he dropped by his parents' house tripping one evening to raid the fridge, he ran smack into two police detectives who'd come to question him about some petty crime. Witnesses had pointed to his photo, among others, in our high school yearbook. It came to nothing, of course, but the unpleasant rush of being questioned by a pair of police while tripping his brains out was profoundly unsettling for him, and he only returned to the Waymore once to pick up his things.

Robbie, while seeming oblivious to the sexual tensions—ignoring the blue paint staining my sheets—and absorbing with an unchanging grin the same doses of chemicals the rest of us took, was no longer my shadow. In my increasingly waspish state, he was an embarrassing reminder of my dorky past and we went our own ways.

I finally lost my grip one night shortly after returning

from my grandfather's funeral in Abilene. Tripping wildly, I kept switching the gooseneck lamp beside my mattress off and it kept spookily clicking back on. An old sepia photo of my great-uncle Tommy Lowry in his sailor uniform, which I'd taken from Grandpa's dresser drawer, kept diving off the table each time I propped it back up. When I looked in the bathroom mirror I saw a skull. I stomped downstairs speaking gibberish and barricaded myself in a cubbyhole under the stairs, where I shuddered and hallucinated for the rest of the night.

I was off the bus. My grim-faced father came to get me and my things in his pickup the next day, leaving the others without a desk, coffee table, or stereo. William watched from the balcony clad in a ragged wizard's cloak someone had filched from the drama department, strewing me with tiny glitter stars as I glumly climbed into the truck and was driven away.

It was a month later that I attempted suicide with a bottle of Anacin, then put falling in love with straight boys away with other childish things and, while finishing my B.A., embarked with a vengeance on a two-year course of such promiscuity as El Paso's couple of back-alley gay bars and two military bases could offer.

Over the years I occasionally heard news of Wayne from Claire, with whom we both kept in touch: marriage, kids, financial struggles. Twenty-two years after I'd last spoken to him, I wrote, through Claire, to say that I'd been thinking about the Waymore days, and to send what I'd written. After several months passed, I realized I wasn't going to be getting a response.

Or was I? Six months later, on one of our long, biannual catch-up phone calls, Claire abruptly said, "Oh, did I tell you about Wayne? He tracked Shelly down on the Internet—she's divorced—and left his wife and went to live with her. It's like something you read about—they just picked up where they left off." So Natalie was the last to bed after all.

This is the part of the story where I'm supposed to slam down the phone, gnash my teeth, and pitch all my pastel sweaters in the floor. But the truth is I'm happy for Wayne. Maybe we'd have stayed friends if I hadn't demanded love or nothing, a circle I wouldn't stop treading till my forties.

Deeper Inside the Valley of Kings

I stood leaning against the wall by the stairs at Sutter's Mill, eating peanuts and drinking a beer. I was feeling a rare surge of confidence: I'd just talked Mrs. Eidenmueller, the blue-haired owner of Bonanza Books, into giving me a fifty-cents-an-hour raise, and earlier, a German tourist who'd been reading a Grove Erotic Classic with a prominent hard on barging around in his shorts had flirted with me at the register.

Sutter's was a San Francisco Financial District bar; it was the middle of the afternoon. Most people there were coming from work or were on their breaks. A cute boy walked over and reached into the peanut barrel, glancing at me. I stared boldly back at him; he looked flustered and moved on, but a minute later he'd thought better of it and came back, standing right beside me. "Work around here?" I said. It was a time when life was a bit of a porn movie.

He told me everything he knew: he drives into the city

once a week for orchestra rehearsal—he plays the oboe; he's a freshman at San Jose State; he's on the wrestling team. He's nineteen, works part-time in a film-developing lab, and collects old cameras. ("You mean they don't even *work?*" I said, unenthusiastically.) I wasn't really listening. If I had been, I might have realized sooner that he was riveting to look at, but dull as a lawn gnome. He *was* cute: on the short side, stocky; from the bulgy crotch to the compact round ass, the contents of his button-flies seemed bent on release. I could imagine his dick snapping to rigidity like an inflatable life preserver. He was wearing a long-sleeved green-and-blue-checked shirt like your mom would buy at Sears (as his no doubt had) and a blue windbreaker with the hood still attached. He looked like he'd just wandered out of the middle row of my eighth-grade class photo.

I had to get back to work. We exchanged names and as I turned to go he put his palm flat against my chest, stopping me to ask what bars I frequented on Castro. It was as if he were feeling for my heart.

A week later I was back at Sutter's on my break, slouched at a table in the half-dark with my legs stretched out. Once in a while a guy would remark on my long, Texan's legs (presumably not meaning bowed), so I indulged my bad posture, throwing out my Dingo boots like bait. I'd forgotten his name, but I remembered that he drove into the city on Mondays. I was about to leave when he appeared: light brown hair parted on the side and swooped across his forehead like a schoolboy's; big, doe-like brown eyes; sturdy thighs. He was smiling broadly: "Kevin?"

This time it really hit me: I was so attracted to him I could hardly speak. He sat on the edge of a chair he pulled up beside me and, looking around the bar, casually let his leg bump mine. My cock stiffened against my jeans, and there was a sort of buzzing in my ears. The boy, whose name was Ben, nattered on about orchestra and his German-language major. I noted that he sometimes affected an ersatz German accent (he lived, for instance, in Zan Oh-zay), but I forgave this small foible instantly. He smelled of baby shampoo and fabric softener, and I wanted to yank down his jeans, stick my tongue up his plump ass, then fuck him hard and fast.

My lust was amplified by confusion: this very specific and overwhelming desire to poke was unusual for me. My experiences with guys back in Texas had mostly been versatile, but over the last two years in San Francisco I'd most often been cast as Boy to a series of late-thirtyish Tarzans. Other than some one-time tricks I hadn't had a relationship with someone my own age or younger. I was accustomed to waking up beside some big, warm, older man who'd stroke my hair back from my forehead and murmur, "Pretty..." "Twenty-one? Twenty-two? Twenty-four?" they'd repeat, when I answered the inevitable awestruck question. "You're just a *baby!*"

My friend Steve would harangue me on the bad deal he felt I was getting from these men. "You mean he doesn't let you fuck *him?* What does he *do,* for chrissakes, just lie back and smoke a cigarette while you jack off?" I hated to admit that that was often exactly what happened. Nick, for example, was selfish, pompous, and lazy, but he looked like Alan Bates and he was as far as you could get from the queers my dad hooted at on television. I might have gone on warming his feet indefinitely if I hadn't finally figured out that his eccentric vocabulary and eerie non sequiturs weren't the result of a mild stroke: he was an est graduate. "What is, *is,* right?" he'd say with a screwy grin. "I'm just an asshole, *okay?*"

Nick looked like Alan Bates; Ben reminded me of Wayne Connor. I was always cruising men who reminded me of one of these romantic icons of my past, and it was always a mistake. For a blissful period I'd be thinking *My God, I'm kissing So-and-So, I'm fucking So-and-So*—but sooner or later I'd find myself staring irritably up from bed at a petulant stranger waving a driver's license in my face, shouting, "I'm just plain Judy Barton, from Salina, Kansas!" like Kim in *Vertigo*.

"I feel like doing something *different* tonight," Ben said, rolling the *R*s like he was Herr Somebody. I brought him home to the half-empty railroad flat I shared with two guys who worked with me at Bonanza: Eddie, a straight boy from Tampa who holed up in his room writing long letters to his former girlfriend or strumming James Taylor songs on his guitar late into the night; and Nate, another gay boy. Nate and I routinely sat on the floor in the unfurnished living room drinking and smoking pot, or went to the Stud on acid and dragged tricks home while Eddie took cover behind his door or went for his daily three-mile run. Eddie was virtuous but sexy, stepping carefully over beer cans and bongs with his bowl of Wheat Chex, and Nate and I guiltily eyed the sweat-soaked blue running shorts he left draped over the shower curtain.

Ben and I climbed up the back stairs to the roof to smoke a joint and look at the view east to the downtown skyline, and before you could say *The Fountainhead*, we were necking like parched men at a spigot and I'd wedged my hand down the back of his jeans, snaking a finger into the damp and mysterious region of his asshole. I pulled him back down to the flat, and we brushed past Eddie in the hall, our shirttails half-out and hard-ons jutting rudely.

He yelped like a puppy when I tried to stick it in. He had his eyes screwed shut and he looked as if he might cry.

"Do you want me to stop?" I said.

"No. No, I want you to fuck me. I've just never done it before."

Shut up in my room, clothes scattered, lying on my unzipped sleeping bag on the bare mattress, I had his stocky, hairy legs pushed back to his head so I could see the dark swirls of hair on his pale chest and the almost-hidden tiny pink nipples. With only the tip of my dick in him, I could just manage to bend and suck hard on the red, blustery head of his cock. He had what my friend Steve called *the doorstop kind*, meaning one of those cast-iron Scotties up on its haunches or a weighted Coke bottle with a knit poodle head—thick and short. I wasn't really inside him yet, I was just nudging my way into the vestibule, his tight ring clenching and grabbing my cockhead. I hadn't yet passed that invisible barrier I knew so well from the other side—that abrupt, melting *give* after which even the largest of cocks could go barreling the rest of the way in without impediment.

His eyes were still closed. "Look at me," I said. I bent and stuck my tongue in his mouth, then pulled back and, still staring into his wide pupils, pushed right up him. He was staring back at me, alternately biting his lip and uttering little *uhs* and *yeuhs*. I was moaning as I sawed in and out, the sweat rolling off my forehead and the end of my nose; I heard Eddie stomp across his room just beyond the sliding pocket doors, pick up his guitar, and start singing "Fire and Rain" in a hopeless attempt to block us out. I threw my whole weight onto Ben, rutting deep and hard, rolling and twisting in him. I felt the cum burning slowly up my cock like the mercury registering a fever on a cartoon thermometer, and I pulled almost but not quite out. I grabbed his jumpy little stump and gave it two or three jerks, and as he lost his last shred of inhibition and shouted "Yeah, *fuck me!*" his cum shot smack against my chin and down my chest and I swiped up a hot gob of it and fed it to him while his spasming asshole wrung from my raw dick the hottest orgasm I'd shot since Joey Carson made me sit on a Coke bottle and masturbate for him in the seventh grade.

Eddie was singing weakly about Carolina and I imagined he wished he were there.

We got up and went out for pizza. Wasn't I already squirming as he held my hand tightly all the way to the restaurant? When he asked, "Could I spend the night?" after we'd gotten back into bed and I'd fucked him again, his tender little asshole still slick from earlier, my dick so hard it felt like a punishment; when we lay soaked and stuck together and he told me what he hadn't till then, that it was his birthday; when he said, through half-shut eyes, "I think I'm falling in love," what iron force seized my resisting jaw and made me utter back, "Me too"?

I *thought* I wanted a lover. The bars on Castro, Polk, Haight, and Folsom were like the pastel-colored squares on the Candy Land board, with LOVER at the end, the pot of gold. I approached every trick as the potential love of my life—but in fact, I relished the exciting, encapsulated event of a one-night stand. *Who am I?* I'd ask myself: I'm this sexy, unknown, completely new person that Jim or Bob or Rick is treating like found money. I'm whoever I tell him I am. Later, of course, he might rise and, donning a caftan, light a cigarette and start to tell you about this really good book he was reading (*Don't Say Yes When You Want to Say No*, or *Reclaiming Your Inner Child of the Past*), or you'd step into the bathroom and find yourself in the stifling dark heart of the Judy Museum, surrounded by chrome-framed blowups of the twitchy, hand-wringing star. Or you might be lying there dewy-eyed and smitten, the cum still cooling on your chest, while he, having sized you up post-orgasm as under-employed disco trash, was yanking on his tight black jeans and, looking meaningfully from his watch to the door, saying, "I've got some calls to make." Whatever the outcome, there was a particular feeling of satiety and exuberance I treasured, walking home sticky and rumpled in last night's clothes, lips swollen and cock chafed.

I'd march right home and, sitting at the table with a cup of coffee, write it all down. It was no coincidence that prior to beginning a journal in college, I'd last kept a little red diary around the time I reached puberty and spent that steamy Texas summer fucking and sucking with Joey, and I'd resumed journal-keeping when I came out at nineteen and began having sex with men again. Sex made me want to write, and I wanted to write about sex.

When we'd kissed good-bye for the last time and he'd backed down the block to his car, waving and smiling sadly, I turned back to the flat, my mind agog. I felt inexpressible relief at being away from Ben after twelve hours of his rapt gaze—and I couldn't wait to see him again. What if he blew me off? *I'm in love*, I thought, to see how it sounded—but a nasty little voice piped up sneeringly from outside the

Deeper Inside the Valley of Kings

Valentine heart: *"Zan Oh-zay?"*

All the pretty ones to the front! Last call at the Stud: the dee-jay's smirky amplified words cut through the earsplitting Blondie ("And if I *do,* will anything happen?"). I'd been thinking about Ben with lust and anxiety all week, but it was Friday night and I could only sit at home mooning over him in my silk-bound China Books diary for so long. Beer-blurry in the jarring brightened lights (*Gentlemen, the bar is now closed!*), I shuffled once around the rectangular bar, kicking trash and cigarette butts, looking.

"You—I'll take *you!*" I turned to see the tall, strapping, Michael Yorkish blond who'd grabbed my arm. "C'mere." We kissed drunkenly. "You're cute—the shy type, right?" One hand played over my crotch; he tilted my face back in the light with the other. I thought he might ask to see my teeth. "How'd you like my big cock up your ass?" he said, halting the flow of traffic around us for a moment. He registered my angry look. "Hey, don't get all insulted. You want to get laid, don't you? Just come home with me; you don't have to do anything you don't want."

The interior of his Camp Street flat looked like the inside of Jeannie's bottle, all dirty velvet and piled drapery. The furniture and windows were gauze- and ruffle-laden, the air thick with patchouli, pot, and the inevitable litter box, and I felt like I'd just stumbled into a musty chamber in the Valley of Kings, as if the walls might be covered with fading hieroglyphs of bird-faced homosexuals walking sideways—but there was no way of knowing if this was the case because every inch of wall was covered with large and small framed photographs of Marilyn in every phase of her career. The cluttered bedroom was dominated by a wrecked canopy bed, swathed in dirty netting, a pith helmet artfully tossed over one post.

Then we were naked and rolling around inside his sultan's tent. He was on top of me, pinning my shoulders with his elbows and kissing me in a way I didn't like, dredging his tongue around my mouth and then slavering my chin and nose with saliva, like a drunk applying lipstick. He'd been grinding what felt like a very large cock against mine, pushing my hand away when I tried to reach for it, and stretching my arms back over my head; now he moved down and took my dick in his mouth and started sucking elaborately, loose and slobbery all the way down and up, and then jacking it with one hand tightly gripping the base and sucking hard on the swollen head. I forgot my momentary annoyance and started thrusting into his mouth. I'd purposely not been jacking off till the next time I'd see Ben, and now I felt a dramatic load on its way.

"Not so fast, cowboy." He flipped me over, spread a gob of Vaseline across the crack of my ass and in with his finger. Then, pushing my face down into the mattress with one hand, he jammed the fat head of his dick inside me and kept on pushing, though I tried to squirm away with a muffled, "Wait a minute, it's hurting...." It was all mechanical then: he was pistoning in and out of me, yanking all the way out and then slamming back in from different angles. Each time I reached for my own cock he grabbed my wrist and wrestled it back to the bed. He seemed not so much to be fucking me as performing the abstract act of fucking someone. I'd relax my way into liking it for a while, and then, after more long minutes of rough pumping, my butt would start to clench up and hurt. Finally he slowed down, ground as far up into me as he could get, and leaned around the side of my head, drooling in my ear. "You're real hot up inside, you know that? I'm gonna fuck you real hard some more, and then I'm gonna squirt a real big load way up inside you, and it's gonna be so much and so hot you're gonna feel it shoot. Now open up for me, baby."

The soreness had abated some while he was still; now he slammed it in and out like a bully jabbing at your shoulder saying, *Yeah, you want to fight, you gonna do something about it?* and my insides were fluttering and out of control and I thought *Christ, I'm going to piss myself* and then some crucial bit of tension broke and I was jutting my ass back to meet his hammer thrusts and he seemed to come straight through me and I was ejaculating, one, two, three, a gush with each lunge and then he yelled and dug into me, arms locked around my chest, shaking and gasping.

"Hey," he said, head propped on his arm, "you're sweet. Why don't you stay and just cuddle awhile?" I was yanking on my socks, my legs shaking, pulling on my *Tom and Jerry* sweatshirt (which showed the cartoon mouse with a little puff of smoke under his running feet) wrong-side-out.

"I really have to go."

He watched me from the bedroom doorway as I started down the hall. "The door's the other way."

"My coat's this way," I said, diving back into the Marilyn gallery, and then finding and fumbling open the front door. He yelled after me from the top of the stairs: "Why don't you do yourself a favor, huh? Just don't go back to the Stud! It's not your style!"

I didn't see Ben for a couple of weeks; he didn't have his regular Monday rehearsal, and I was busy finding and moving into a studio apartment on Polk Street, after Nate went back to Michigan to finish college and Eddie returned to Tampa to get married, his love letters having won the day. We'd talked on the phone several times—short, halting conversations consisting chiefly of sentiments like "I really want to see you" and long sighs. I imagined Ben practicing his oboe or arranging his camera collection after we hung up, or writing me one of those Hallmark cards I'd been getting regularly ("Just thinkin' of you...") with "Love, Ben" down at the bottom. In my diary or in conversation with any friend who'd put up with listening, I debated whether or not I was in love. Other nights I walked out to the Giraffe or the Cinch and tricked.

I couldn't wait to get him alone in my new apartment. We met at Sutter's, grinning like idiots. He looked freshly showered and glowing, dressed in stiff new Levi's and another plaid shirt, this one brown and green. "Let's go by my place first," I said. We were kissing and pulling at each other's clothes as soon as we got through the door. I crouched, unbuckled his belt, opened his pants, wedged out his fat cock, and started sucking it hungrily. He leaned against the wall, eyes shut, breathing deeply. He started to pull me up, but I pushed his hands away. "It may take me a long time to come like this."

"That's okay," I said, and went back to work, jacking it with my thumb and forefinger and slurping on the head, tugging lightly on his heavy balls. I had the unfamiliar sensation of debauching a youth—though in fact he was only a couple of years younger than me—because his Jockeys smelled slightly of talcum powder, because he was so awkward and inexperienced. After maybe ten minutes, his legs started to quiver and he clutched at the sides of my head, hanging on to my ears—"Oh jeez, you're gonna make me"—and my mouth was flooded with pungent sperm that tasted of modeling clay. He sank down to kiss me but I pushed him lower to the carpet.

"Let me see your ass," I said. He was all tangled up in his jeans, which were only pulled down just past the curve of his buttocks. I'd been jacking my cock while I blew him; now I stroked it slowly over his pale, plump, damp butt, which was half-obscured by his shirttail and white T-shirt. His crack smelled sweet and just slightly funky, its fuzz of black hair plastered down with sweat. I spit several times into my palm and stroked my dick, scooted onto him with the open fly of my jeans pressing at the base of my scrotum, and pushed it slowly up him. "Aww man, aww man," he muttered as I stretched myself full-length, skewering him, turning his head so we could kiss. His asshole felt tight and rough with just the spit for lube, and I kept my thrusts deep inside him, reaching under his hips to pull him closer against me. After that I was just pumping and kissing his neck while he lay still and shivered each time I thrust, goose bumps rising on his sweat-slicked back. Then the semen came jerking out of me, and I lay breathing on top of him, separate, shaken from a violent dream, the taste of his spunk still sharp on my tongue.

"I don't have class again till Wednesday. Can I stay over?"

"Sure."

"I love you."

Later, after going out to dinner, we both sat with notebooks on our laps, writing, though I found I couldn't be very frank in my journal with Ben shifting and sighing a few feet away. I glanced over, and couldn't help noticing something strange about his loopy printing. He looked up. "I write in German, for practice," he said.

He was still there when I came home from work the next day. "My car wouldn't start. I took it to a Datsun place on Van Ness. Guess I'll just have to miss class tomorrow."

Two days later, his car repaired, Ben went home. "In a way, I'm almost glad my generator went out, because I got to spend all this time with you."

"Uh-huh," I answered. I was walking him down Polk Street to his car, and I wondered if anyone I knew in the Giraffe would be looking out as we went by holding hands. I felt guilty and crabby, shocked at my own brisk transformation: three nights of adoring glances and camera talk, of Ben poring over and underlining passages in his copy of *Loving Someone Gay*—three nights of unrelieved Daddyhood—had killed my sexual obsession. Whatever I'd been projecting onto him had dissolved, leaving behind a clinging stranger. He was just plain Judy Barton, from Salina, Kansas.

"I've never been so happy," he said with a misty smile as he got into his car.

"Talk to you soon," I said, almost looking behind me for the long, scaly tail. I'd put him out of my mind before I got a block away. A hustler standing in front of the Bagel Deli with a torn tank top and a snootful of speed stared at me appraisingly. Both our heads jerked as a horn beeped a few yards away: Ben, frantically waving one more good-bye.

I got another one of his cards the very next day: "Words are coming easier to me now. You've brought so much into my life...."

I dodged Ben's phone calls all week and distracted myself with an old fuck-buddy, Dennis. Dennis would call up every couple of months, I'd bus over to his Mission flat, and I'd fuck him or he'd fuck me. He was in his late thirties, skinny, with thinning hair and glasses, but he was kind, funny, undemanding, and he fucked with the attention and passion of an aging man who takes nothing for granted.

I lay stretched out lazily on Dennis's bed, staring at the red lights on the Twin Peaks tower blinking through the condensation on the tall windows, reaching for another slug of Budweiser while he sucked on my cock. Dennis's straight-boy fantasy of me almost required that I be lazy and selfish; I could lie back and be ravished. When he pushed my legs back over my shoulders and fucked me, it was long and slow and sweet.

The following Monday I agreed to meet Ben at Sutter's. "You seem bummed out," he said, trying to take my hand. We went straight to the Grub Stake for dinner; I sat glumly while he chattered about his job, his classes. "I've told my parents I may start spending weekends with a friend in the city," he said. "Hey, what's wrong? Are you mad at me?"

"It's not your fault," I lied. "I just get depressed. That's why I'm living alone. I just need to be by myself sometimes."

Then I stopped returning his calls.

I got a letter from him after a couple of weeks, block-printed on a sheet of lined notebook paper: "I never knew anybody could be as cruel as you. You've broken my heart. I hope you really do love somebody someday and he hurts you like you've hurt me."

Dennis lay panting on top of me, sweat and cum coating our chests. My eyes filled up suddenly and a couple of tears spilled out. "Sweetheart," he said, pushing my hair back from my forehead, kissing my closed eyes while I sobbed. "Sweetheart."

One Saturday morning six weeks later, the phone rang as the door clicked shut behind Dennis. "Hello! Is this *Uncle* Kevin?" I lay on my stomach listening to Mom in Texas talking excitedly about the birth of my older brother's first child. "Yeah?" I said. "That's great. How many pounds?" I heard the apartment door swing open. Dennis must have forgotten something, I figured. I half-turned, hand over the mouthpiece. Ben, staring at me impassively, was kneeling at the foot of the mattress. "I'll be off in a second," I said, thinking I'd better get him out where there were other people. "Let me just get some clothes on and we can go somewhere and talk as soon as—"

"*Nein.*" He was unbuckling his belt, pulling open his button-flies, a strange little determined smirk I didn't recognize on his face. I shook my head emphatically and started to pull the sheet up. He yanked it out of my hand, shoved me back onto my stomach, and threw his weight on top of me, one arm in a serious choke hold around my neck.

"I don't know if we're driving to Abilene for this year's Stone family reunion or not..." The receiver was now mashed against my face. "It'll just be a bunch of fat people standing around a graveyard talking about dead people." I still had a crazy half-idea Ben just wanted a hug. When he pushed a wet finger up my butt, I struggled in earnest to throw him off, but he'd locked his thighs around me and was making it difficult for me to breathe.

And then, amazingly, he rammed his fat, short, plunger of a dick in my asshole with one rough movement and started humping fast without another word, never releasing his hold on my neck. I'd dropped him because his passivity bored me; his neediness had been a terrifying mirror. Who was this aggressive stranger?

"Daddy's having those security bars installed on all the windows; I said it's like *we're* in prison, but he wants to do it, so that's that—what are you doing, washing dishes while I'm talking?"

You can tell when someone's fucking you with tenderness, however brutally he may be socking it in, and when his whole excitement is a kind of contempt. This was something new I couldn't place. Ben was jabbing his dick in with cold precision, but his death-grip on me conveyed something else. It was uncomfortable; he was *hurting* me, he was telling me something I didn't want to hear. I felt as if he were trying to break me open and peer inside.

Do You Believe
I Love You?

When I saw him on the street that day, a hollow-eyed, shuffling Nosferatu, I knew he'd be turning up in the trickle of
obits in the *Bay Area Reporter* before you could say Coming
Home Hospice. I hadn't seen Sam in fifteen years; if I'd
thought of him recently, I'd have assumed he was already
dead, or had moved back to Tennessee.

We don't die of love, of course, though for a very long
while there a lot of us were popping off regularly from something tragically associated with it. I came near to dying of
love for Sam, though, or thought I did—twice.

It's said that many gay men in the seventies and early
eighties were attempting to lead the lives of boy-crazy teenage
girls they'd envied in their own adolescences. This was true of
me. I was a twenty-five-year-old man employed as a paperback
buyer in a downtown San Francisco bookstore; but standing
behind the register, bellying up to a bar, or jumping about on

a blinking dance floor, I still saw myself as that brainy, well-behaved sixteen-year-old, the sedate Hayley twin in *The Parent Trap*, ready to worship slavishly at the altar of the first self-assured, not-so-smart, sexually aggressive guy who chose to take off my glasses and pull me down onto a dirty mattress.

My journal of tricks and affairettes was fairly cold-blooded, but tellingly I had cut out and glued on the flyleaf a campy frame from a romance comic of a girl weeping into her pillow beneath the legend: *And sometimes, even when I just dreamed about Bill with another girl, I cried in my sleep.* It was July of '81 and I had just reread the complete novels of Jean Rhys—so it should have come as no surprise that when a slim, hard, ex-sheet-metal worker from Tennessee sidled up to me one Sunday at the End-Up and asked me to dance, my smart mouth and good sense evaporated in the heat of his blue gaze and I entered on an ecstatic and painful interval of utter, craven bondage.

My life has been parsed by Sundays. Depressing memories of forced marches to Baptist church and Sunday school back in El Paso are never completely banished—along with the hateful boredom of our stale suburban tract house afterward as my parents napped, or played Aggravation at the kitchen table.

In my senior year of high school, Sundays had been spent driving around aimlessly partying with my straight doper pals; this had morphed to tripping and hanging out with the Waymore gang. Then came life in Mecca, and Sundays were either an Elysium of lazy days in bed or at the movies with the latest boyfriend, or an existential nightmare of staring at the phone and weeping, trying to pretend that lying on the couch all evening reading an Iris Murdoch novel cover to cover constituted a life.

If you passed through Friday and Saturday nights without meeting someone, or if, as was the case with my best friends Gary and Michael, you weren't getting along that well with the lover you had, Sunday afternoons and evenings were the worst. Michael would call me up to go dancing at noon. "What else were you planning to do, slit your wrists?" he'd ask in his world weary Florida drawl.

Michael and Gary got me into the habit of going down to the End-Up on Sundays, or *church*, as everyone called it, with a nod to our common Sunday phantoms. We'd meet at Powell and Market and go racing down Sixth Street, stepping around passed-out drunks, broken beer bottles, and pools of urine. Approaching Sixth and Harrison I felt the bass throb at the same moment as I saw the ugly brown-trimmed building with the crooked white plastic letters. That first glimpse always made me think of the Sugar Bowl Nightclub in *Fearless Fly* cartoons—the walls physically pulsing with the music and swelling as the syncopated patrons streamed in.

When you stepped inside you felt the chill of ice—ice in bins behind the big rectangular bar, crushed ice regularly dumped into the steaming urinals—and warring with this, the wet, insinuating heat of the big raised dance floor, where people with flushed damp faces, or sunken-eyed, tripping-all-night faces of a gray pallor, stomped and spun and windmilled their arms. We'd dance, drink thirty-five-cent draft beer from plastic cups, sit outside in the sun drying off, and then dance again till our T-shirts were stained white with salt and our hair stuck out however it dried. For those hours I was happy: laughing, confident of my looks and at ease in my body; delivered from the Sunday horrors.

As anyone who drinks and has taken recreational drugs

can tell you, when it's fun, it's great fun, and when it goes wrong, it's awful. Many of those Sundays ended badly, when I'd drink too many beers and stalk out after cross words with Gary or Michael, sleepwalking into the parking meters along Sixth Street. Or I'd swallow some offered capsule with youthful insouciance and later, too high for speech or eye contact, rush home in terror and ride it out in bed with the blinds down, ready to swear off everything if I could only have my sharp, sober mind back again. On those convalescent evenings, the hypnotic ticking of the *60 Minutes* stopwatch on a poorly-tuned black-and-white TV gave a kind of soul balm.

It was on one of the happy days that I noticed Sam eyeing me. "Do you know what a beautiful smile you have?" he said, leaning up close in the loud bar, and I was aware only of his clear blue eyes, his shiny, straight white teeth, and the fact that he was drenched with sweat and yet he smelled good—ferny, fecund, like clean but damp privates.

Gary, nearby, was less starstruck. "You smell dick, you mean. That guy *lives* here. He's a lying sack of shit with all that corn pone sincerity. You'd better look out."

We danced together for several hours. Sitting out back against the high fence that blocked a freeway ramp, we drank foaming, tepid beers, while people around us shrieked with laughter or restlessly cruised.

His name was Sam Warren, he was thirty years old, and he'd only come to San Francisco from Tennessee a few months before, leaving behind an ex-wife and two little boys—but he wanted to get custody of the kids and bring them out to California, he said. While I was telling him about myself he leaned over and deftly licked my wet forehead. Then he kissed me, and I gave myself over to kissing back, with ridiculously pounding heart and hollow stomach. When he broke away and returned to his cigarette with a satisfied smile, the first thing I saw was Gary, glaring at me from across the patio like a gargoyle.

We didn't go home together till the following Sunday, which gave me a week to wonder if he'd really show up again, and whether my impression of him wasn't utterly misremembered. As with all divine visitations I'd been blinded, and I couldn't really recall his face—only how I'd felt.

He did come, and in the early evening I brought him back to my studio above the Stockton Steps. When we'd sat a few minutes on the old green vinyl couch and he'd smoked a cigarette, he leaned back and smiled crookedly at me, stretching his legs out. It was twilight, with only a little light filtering through the ivy framing the one big window. In the amber glow of the brass floor lamp his delicate features, golden mustache, and longish light brown hair reminded me of the *Mud Slide Slim*-era James Taylor.

"Take your clothes off," he said quietly. Outside the fog had begun to roll in, the foghorns were doing their muffled bellowing, and as I pulled off my purple high-tops and T-shirt and jeans, I started to tremble. We kissed, then he pushed me off and stood up. "Take it out," he said, staring hard at me. I fumbled his belt buckle and stiff new button-flies open.

Maybe Gary was right and I *had* been smelling dick. It was very erect. It stuck straight out and up, jerking when I touched it—and gave off a slightly sweet, mushroomy, mulchy odor, attributable, I thought, to the bit of pale retracted hood. It wasn't especially large, but as befitted the most beautiful man I'd ever seen, he had what seemed to me a perfect penis: marble-white, smooth and hard, not bumpy and gristly, with a just-discernible blue vein pulsing beneath the skin right up to the corona, and a thick flushed head, all pointing up and jabbing at the air like a gesturing dictator.

The exhaustive range of that first night's lovemaking was quickly honed to the essential. On those few occasions when I was allowed to penetrate Sam, he lay motionless on his stomach, fists clenched, and endured with a sort of grim air of accomplishment. His "top" abilities were subtler and more erotic than the overt professionalism of the left-hankeyed muscle queens (who danced with stiff chopping and squatting motions, as if moving phantom weights). Sam swung his hips and wrists unself-consciously on the dance floor, and he fucked like it was as necessary as breathing, raining kisses and endearments onto me with an almost feminine hysteria. Up till now I'd wanted my partners to clam up during sex, nothing turning me off faster than a stream of unconvincing porno-movie dialogue ("Yeah, take that Big Daddy Dick!"). Yet while Sam fucked me, or as we drifted off to sleep folded into each other, he uttered the most intense expressions of need and tenderness I'd ever heard. I hadn't had such romantic sex with a man before, and it bowled me over.

A twist that quickly brought me to a state of both resentment and helpless, slobbering attraction, like the hypnotist's subject in a cartoon, was Sam's out-of-bed stance that sex was the thing I needed, like a sick boy needs his medicine, to be doled out patiently and deliberately. I soon learned well enough that Sam's galloping sex drive (and everything else) took second place to his love for drugs, preferably administered through a needle, yet it irked me that someone clearly in need of lots of sex, who had to have it and went out compulsively looking for more of it when he wasn't with me, kept up the charade that I was insatiably trying to "get a piece" off him.

Looking at Sam's tall, wiry frame; the sixties schoolboy side part and the light brown bangs hanging across his eyes; the untucked, tapered plaid Sears shirts, sleeves rolled up to the elbow; the badness and swagger—I was overcome with a devotion that went straight back to my adolescence. Sam embodied my older brother and every other hood who'd ever cupped his crotch and sneered at me. He was no good: everyone said so, he said so himself, part of his rap when he got high. "You're gettin' too serious about me, honey. I love you, but I'm afraid you're gonna get hurt. You'll hate me one day."

Sam had a sidekick and caretaker, Harlan, who had preceded him in an earlier scouting party of gay men from Nashville, and who had also found him his job as a maintenance man at a huge mall outside the city. (I never let myself even think the word *janitor*. Besides, he made more than I did selling books, and I wasn't averse to having a boyfriend who stood around at work in a light green uniform with *Sam* stitched in red cursive writing over the same pocket that held his pack of Kool menthols—who popped a tall malt liquor as he came through the door, and fretted about being late with his child support.) Harlan was plump and not always quite clean, speaking confidentially in my ear with a sour beer breath while his big, slightly jaundiced eyes constantly ticked over the passing men. He had the evil chuckle of a much fatter man, and an almost unintelligible drawl, like a disco Burl Ives. Gary, who made lurid faces behind his back at the End-Up, dubbed him The Stewed Chicken because of his pigeon chest, and the way he looked as if you could detach one of his greasy limbs by simply pulling on it. Harlan wheezed about Sam's bad exploits over the kitchen table while we both pretended we didn't know Sam was shooting up in his bedroom, or at my side in a dance bar while I nervously watched to see who Sam was dancing with now.

Harlan filled me in on Sam's departure from Tennessee. He'd been shooting up speed and MDA so often, he got fired from his job with an exterminator—another green-jumpsuit position—amid threats of prosecution for stealing prescription drugs from clients' medicine cabinets. He attempted suicide with some of his booty, but was saved at the last moment by Harlan, who nursed him back to functional health, and brought him out to San Francisco after extracting a short-lived oath that he'd never shoot up again.

We fell into seeing each other regularly, usually spending Thursday through Sunday nights together, always Sunday afternoons at the End-Up. Though Sam had vigorously pursued me, I soon found that for all his talk of love, he was not to be pressed for the slightest commitment. He considered us both entirely free to have sex with others whenever we liked. "Do you want to know how many guys I've been with since I met you?" he asked after the first month, to my horror. "I'm not gonna lie to you." Sam didn't approve of jealousy. "I better not ever catch you acting jealous, or that'll be all she wrote!" How could he love me as much as he crooned in my ear each night, how could he phone me every day to tell me so and call me his little pumpkin nose, and then bring someone else home? Besotted and obsessed, I still knew that I held a minority viewpoint in 1981 San Francisco, and I tried to believe that I was being childish and unreasonable.

Most of the time, I came to Sam's place to spend the night. The Victorian flat he shared, with its tilting, creaking floorboards beneath the cheap carpet, had been gutted in a fire, and the quick makeover hadn't banished the acrid smell of charred wood and mold that seeped from behind the new paint. The odor, the marginal Hayes Valley side street, and the troubled lives of Harlan and the other occupants lent an air of impending disaster, orchestrated with sirens and car alarms. The fainting room that served as his bedroom had just enough space for a double bed and the giant birdcage that held his white cockatiel. (I suspected that in his first weeks in the city he'd been one of those *Swiss Family Robinson* clones you used to see strutting around with unsanitary-looking parrots on their shoulders.) Sam was no more responsible a pet owner than he was a parent; I never saw him take the bird out or feed it, though there was food, or the cracked husks of it, spread over every surface in the room. I'd wake in the icy night to the screech and flap of the bird, Sam flipping on the overhead light in time for us to see mice diving from the bottom of the cage and running in all directions. He would sit up and smoke a cigarette then, my head on his hip, stroking my hair and mumbling his litany of endearments: "Honey—you scare me, you know that? My little petunia nose," while bottles smashed and screams rose from the alley beyond the dark window dripping with condensation.

I stared at that same high, rattling window the day I let him shoot me up. It was a cool, foggy Saturday morning. Sam had been in vibrating good spirits the night before; he'd scored a bunch of crystal at work and had already hit up twice in one of his subterranean hiding places at the mall before he got on BART to head home. I woke to find him propped on his elbow and smoking ruminatively, staring down at me.

"Do you know how much I love you?" he said. "You're going to shoot up with me, okay? I'll only give you a little." He got up, locked the door, and dug the green metal toolbox out from under the dirty clothes piled in the closet. I'd watched him do it often enough. He melted the crystal in a spoon with a little water, tied off my arm, and filled a clean syringe, holding it up to the light and tapping it reverently. I felt overwhelming love, coupled with terror. I felt I was letting him take my life, and I wanted to let him do it. He pushed his smoky tongue in my mouth for a moment, then sat back and stuck me.

I was looking away from the needle, staring at his handsome, intent face. Then sudden heat illuminated me like an atomic flash, and with supreme effort I turned my head to see the window where so much light was coming from. A high-frequency buzz started up in my ears and continued down my spine and the wall and window blew in and snapped in my face like wash on a line, and I thought, *This must be what dying is like.* For a while I wasn't even aware of Sam, who quickly injected himself and lay beside me on the bed. The next thing I noticed was a sharp, funky odor: that was us, both shivering and bathed in a sweat so profound even the soles of my feet were slick.

Being with Sam—being in love with him, taking drugs with him—comprised a whole other existence from the life I lived away from him. Around Sam I was ecstatic and apprehensive; I was The Boyfriend, but for how long? Ivy Street, the omnipresent disco mixes, the disco-bunny culture of his few friends and roommates, all were in stark contrast to my Stockton Street studio, bookstore friends, and the Elvis Costello and Go-Go's I listened to. I *was* Heathcliff all right, but my Heathcliff stood in a copse of barstools, and instead of the wind whistling over the moors there was only the thump and falsetto of "Disco Man."

Most of the story was played out on his turf: the slanting-floored Ivy flat, the End-Up, another seedy morning-after bar called the Balcony. He wouldn't come over for dinner, wouldn't meet my friends. If I said yes to some outing with my own friends on a weekend night, I'd spend the evening imagining Sam out getting high and tricking with someone. Away from him, I'd taken to bursting into inappropriate tears, like the tiresome, sobbing girl being ministered to in the back bedroom of every junior high party, distraught because her steady had taken back his ID bracelet and was slow-dancing to "Hey, Jude" with someone else. If I was reckless enough to ask about his evening the next day, Sam would bluntly confess. He'd warned me, hadn't he? "I'll just hurt you, honey!"

Harlan half-heartedly provided cover on those awkward occasions when I called and Sam was actually with someone else. After this happened a few times I began to find it difficult to get high around Sam. I'd never kept up with him anyway and now, whether it was just smoking a joint at his place or swallowing a capsule of MDA outside the End-Up, my jealous worries were difficult enough to handle after even a few beers, and I had to be careful. We'd start out affectionate and smiling, but now every encounter, particularly at the bars, ended mournfully. He'd disappear for too long, and I'd finally find him in a corner with some guy, slipping a phone number into his pocket. "Don't look at me like that," he'd say. "I told you what I was like."

Sometimes he'd call up unexpectedly and ask me to rush over. The passionate love-talk still spilled from him during sex, but now it sounded almost belligerent, as if he were daring me to call him a liar. Now when he shot up in front of me, he'd roll his dilated eyes balefully, like a vampire caught slipping back into his coffin. "You're lookin' at me like I was a bug under a microscope," he'd sigh.

I can't have been more than six years old when my pretty teenage Aunt Janet broke up with her boyfriend Chris. She slashed her hand breaking the glass in his framed senior picture, cut up the bloodied photo with a pair of scissors, and flushed it down the toilet. Later, I traced with my finger where her best friend Patty had written in cursive swirls over a yearbook photo of Janet gazing sadly off Scenic Drive, "Don't jump, Janet. Chris will come back." I swooned, and knew I'd be scorched by love one day.

Lying in bed, Sam told me in awed tones about his younger sister Lisa, whose husband cracked up when she left him. He showed up one day with a gun and made Lisa strip while he rattled off her infidelities, their two toddlers crying and clinging to her legs. Then he put the gun in his mouth and pulled the trigger.

There was drama—public tears! Storming out of bars! We fought one Saturday and I ran out of his place, slamming the door and heading straight for Polk Street, where I got drunk, *bad news* stamped across my forehead, in hopes of trumping Sam's next infidelity. Passed out later, I didn't answer the phone when it rang, and he charged over and shouldered open my studio door. "I thought you might've tried something crazy," he said—a little let down, I thought—and bent me over the foot of the bed while I was still sniffling and wiping my nose on my sleeve. This was both the hottest sex we ever had, and the precise moment when I knew, behind my delusion, that Sam's strange amalgam of desire and contempt for me had reached its zenith. It was the "Every time I kissed you, I had to wipe my mouth!"

moment, as friends and I used to say to each other, mimicking Bette in *Of Human Bondage*.

It wasn't all Mr. Hyde. He used to phone his kids on Saturday mornings, speculating sadly after he hung up as to when he might be able to bring them out. I tried to imagine living somewhere with Sam and helping to parent two shell-shocked little boys, but it was a stretch. He could lie on the couch with an arm thrown around my neck, smoking and watching sitcom reruns with a look of rapt concentration, for hours. But these times, when the omnipresent disco wasn't beating from speakers in every room, when somebody wasn't spreading out coke or crystal on a Thelma Houston album cover at the kitchen table, when Sam wasn't bug-eyed and telling me I'd hate him one day, were rare.

We met in July; by October things were grim. He spent a paycheck on MDA and I didn't see him for a week. I begged him to come over. When he arrived, he sat down on the couch, pulled up his pants leg, and brought out the rig he'd tucked in his sock. "Do you really need to do that?" I asked. He looked at me with infinite fatigue and patience.

"I love you—do you know that? Do you realize how much I love you? Don't you know what you're doin' to me?"

Later, when we took off our clothes and got into bed, I flinched at the dark hematoma blooming on his arm. He was sweating profusely, too exhausted to get hard. After jerking me off mechanically, he passed out. I lay awake trying to cradle him in our accustomed spoon fashion, but he shuddered and kicked, punching at me in his sleep.

Halloween night: As I rode the crowded bus over to Hayes and Laguna, I felt a clear sense of doom about Sam. We'd broken up and gotten back together several times in the last month, one of us buckling each time and calling when the other toughed it out. We'd agreed to spend Halloween together; my old friend Steve and his boyfriend, Billy, were driving up from Monterey. They liked Sam because he liked to go dancing and could always get MDA, and they lectured me for being jealous. "He loves you, anyone can see that. Stop being so possessive!"

When I walked into the flat, the disco was thumping and the place was full of the roommates' boyfriends and friends pacing around, passing joints and drinking beers. I could tell Sam had shot up—he was jittery and joking, smiling at me sheepishly now and then with a quick little nod or wink. Harlan looked at me sympathetically. "You can do a lot better than him, you know," he breathed in my ear. It occurred to me that he knew Sam was already seeing someone else.

Steve and Billy arrived, and we swallowed capsules of MDA—this was Halloween, after all—and headed for the End-Up. It was odd being there at night; I'd only seen its false-twilit Sunday afternoons. We danced in the jam-packed throng. Sam disappeared for long periods and I was too high and occupied with Steve and Billy to bother looking for him. At two we moved on to an after-hours club where for a long stretch I stood gripped between Sam's knees as he sat on a ledge with his arms around my chest, turning my head to be kissed now and then. In these moments, I had what I most wanted.

We got back to the flat and crashed at dawn. I woke only a couple of hours later to see Sam injecting himself in the chill morning air, the green toolbox open on the floor. He and Harlan were headed back to the End-Up for the 8:00 A.M. "Leftovers" party. In the early light the sight of blood rising into the syringe made my balls retract. He cupped my face in his shaking hands. "You know I love you more than anything? You know that, right?"

Around eleven, Steve woke me, and he and Billy and I went back to my place to shower and eat breakfast. If we were up to it, we said, we'd catch up with Sam and Harlan in the afternoon. Driving to the bar several hours later, Billy remembered he'd left his coat at Sam's, and we detoured by Ivy to pick it up. Nobody answered the buzzer, but the door was open, and I bounded up the stairs. The first thing I saw was a dazed-looking blond guy sitting at the kitchen table in his underwear. "Um, hi...?" he said.

"Who's that, Ricky?" Sam called from the bedroom. I pulled Billy's coat off a chair, and plunged back down the stairs.

"Take me home," I said. While Steve and Billy bickered ("But I don't see why we can't go back to the End-Up!"), I hugged my knees in the backseat trying to remember Natalie's voice-over lines from Wordsworth as she drove away from white trash Warren Beatty's farmhouse in *Splendor In the Grass*, a parable of bad love absorbed so early I'd thought it was *splinter*. Bottom had turned back into a man, and I wept bitterly at my release.

Weeks passed. I went to work and shelved paperbacks. At night, I stayed in and read, or went out to Polk and Castro bars with Gary and Michael, who were glad to have me back. Sooner or later I'd come home alone and throw myself on the couch and cry till my nose ran and my head ached. I started *After Leaving Mr. Mackenzie* again. *Sometimes, even when I just dreamed about Sam with another boy, I cried in my sleep.*

Sam had needed a witness, and it wasn't easy to tear my eyes away from the broken glass and crumpled bodies. A film loop of the flat on Ivy and Sam's room with the squawking bird flickered constantly in the back of my mind. I could see the stoned blond lying on the bed while Sam, grim and pale, heated crystal in a spoon and shot up. I could see Sam framing that blond's face with both hands like he'd held mine as he came on to the speed or MDA, nearly passing out, the words tumbling from the drowning man's lips: "Do you believe I love you? Do you believe me?"

Then he phoned me at work one day. "Well hey there! It's Sam! How're you doin', honey?" He sounded sweet, anxious to talk to me. My stomach dropped; I put the phone back in the receiver and sat down on a box of books, Olivia de Havilland heading up the stairs while Montgomery Clift pounded on the bolted door.

He didn't call again. I stayed away from the End-Up and the Balcony after that, so I didn't run into him. I saw Harlan once in a bar several years later. "He ain't doing so good," he said, without my asking.

When I saw him moving in slow motion down the opposite side of Castro Street, my stomach didn't turn over and my legs didn't give the way they once did at the thought of him, but the street between us yawned like the Rio Grande Gorge. Wheeling in that gaping space were two lovers, both dead of AIDS, and the very different requited love and bone grief that had meant. A stream snaked along the bottom of the canyon; that was fifteen years of going on living instead of dying for love, or grief. And stretched swaying across, held by a few ancient, frayed ropes, one of those jungle bridges from *The Lost World*, full of dangerous gaps and likely to snap at any step: the chance of loving again with the tender, stupid heart of a girl.

My Clementina

There's always been hot blood between us. It started shortly after I arrived in San Francisco in 1977 at twenty-one. That first trip to the city clinic was like a straight boy's pilgrimage to a prostitute. It was a rite of gay manhood; you earned your spurs. You took the six-inch cotton swab up your dick or butt and the two fat hypodermics or pills like a man, drank Perrier for five days and caught up on your reading—and the next weekend hit the ground running at the 'N Touch or the Stud. It had a seedy location, the doom smell of Lysol and rubbing alcohol, and the name of a Gold Rush whore: Clementina.

"What happened to you last week?" someone would ask when you reappeared.

"Clementina."

My face would assume a rueful expression as I walked to the VD clinic at Clementina and Fourth in the cool morning air, frightened but proud to be bad. Leaving behind the respectable financial-district throngs, I'd pass empty, chain-link-fenced lots (today's Yerba Buena Center), the ancient, lost-looking red-brick hulk of St. Patrick's, the gaping hole that would be Moscone Center. Inside the nondescript stucco building and up a flight of stairs, the waiting room teemed with love's nervous martyrs, pacing or seated on rows of multicolored plastic chairs.

It had the atmosphere of a rowdy detention hall—electric, shameful, defiant. A couple screaming recriminations could make it sordid; a black queen sweeping out of a treatment room ("And I say, 'Girlfriend, you are *not* stickin' that thing in me!'") could unite the crowd in revolutionary laughter.

In the first moneyless weeks before I found a job, I'd sold plasma half a dozen times at a Tenderloin plasma center. Surrounded by red-eyed drunks and TV hookers, I lay on a table for two hours composing baleful poems (*At this drive-in/patrons sell entrance to lank veins...*) while a pint of red-black blood was siphoned into a plastic pouch, taken away and separated from its straw-colored plasma, and then, chilled and dense, slowly returned to my vein at the end of an icy needle.

I gladly stopped selling plasma when I got a job at Bonanza Inn, a forty-year-old financial district bookstore. There I was taken in hand by Steve, an older (thirty-one) gay man who quickly became my big brother, mentor, and best friend. He stood behind the register box at the bookstore, which was raised up five inches from the checkerboard linoleum like a pulpit, and silently preached from *The Book of Dick*, rating men as they browsed the remainder tables beneath the faded Day-Glo orange *Bargain!* pennants, and buzzing me up to the front for anyone special.

I'd pick up the staticky black intercom phone in the shipping room to hear Steve's sotto voce "Psychology—halfway down the aisle. I think I'm in love."

Steve and I had sex a couple of times, then he tossed me into the deep end and returned to the hunt. Each morning as we emptied the creaking book cart and dissed the latest best sellers, we'd compare notes on the previous evening's adventures, sounding like a couple of jaded tarts.

"You trick?"

"*Jesus*—did I trick? I don't know how I'm *standing* here! It had to be the biggest cock I've ever seen!" Talking to Steve about his conquests was like collecting folklore—you just listened and appreciated, you didn't doubt. They always had dicks of Paul Bunyan dimensions or perfect asses, unless they didn't, and then he could be scathing: "It was like my little *finger*, and naturally he wanted to fuck me! Jesus! It was like lying under a goddamn sewing machine!"

I learned about the clap. Steve would come slamming through the swinging shipping-room door lighting a cigarette, and seconds later come stomping out of the toilet: "Well, I *knew* it! I'm dripping again!" When it came to gonorrhea, Steve was as full of superstition as an old peasant woman. For a while he swore that fucking short, cute, bubble-butted blonds in painter's pants guaranteed you a dose. He was certain a particularly virulent bout of anal gonorrhea he got was directly traceable to a pair of god-like Greek twins he met at the Liberty Baths—Castor and Pox, he called them with a grimace.

One of Steve's theories was that if you tricked with someone and you really hit it off and you started seeing each other, the first serious talk you were likely to have would be when one of you gave the other the clap. To balance out my new life as a Polk Street slut, I'd started going to a community college poetry workshop one night a week, attended chiefly by bored yuppie couples, aging Beats, and pert Emily Dickinson wannabes.

Poems with lines like *As I fucked him, his entrails fluttered like crazed colonists at a maypole...* left my listeners glassy-eyed and speechless, but they got me a ride home with the handsome instructor. Jonah was a tall, clever, bright-eyed and black-goateed poet (with a day job in accounting), and we'd been eyeing each other since the first class. There was something in the haste with which he declared his devotion after our first encounter that made me a little wary, but the sex *was* passionate. A couple of days later I was peeing through broken glass and oozing a nasty pus, and Steve was almost teary-eyed with filial pride. "You really like this guy, don't you?" he said, giving my shoulder a little punch. "See what I told you?"

That was my first time at the clinic, and I went down nobly, in the throes of a new romance. I squeezed my glans over a lab slide and bared my ass for two thigh-numbing shots of penicillin that left me wobbly-legged and dizzy. Jonah was calling to notify me when I got home; he'd been to his private doctor that morning. "The *city clinic?*" he said in horror. "Oh, you poor baby!"

Over the next several years, my dance card—literally a lined index card—at Clementina filled up. Sometimes the tickle and drip would only be urethritis, or "strain"; sometimes I'd be summoned, having been reported as a "contact" by some temporarily diseased sex partner. When diagnosed with gonorrhea, you had to sit in a sour little room with a counselor, a calendar spread out in front of you, and try to match names and phone numbers with the previous ten days—seldom a simple task.

In May of 1979, I came stumbling home drunk one evening and tricked with a previously unmet neighbor in the building's narrow and jerky elevator. We rode to the roof with our pants around our ankles and took turns fucking each other in the gravel, fired up by the smoky tumult and sirens of the White Night riots at Civic Center several blocks away.

There was a line of men reading newspapers and drinking coffee waiting for the clinic to open when I made my way there the following week, suffering both "fore" and "aft," as clinic shorthand put it. Inside, it was like the booking room after a big bust. *"Did you riot?"* someone shouted to a friend. An ill-tempered doctor kept growling conflicting instructions to "spread both cheeks!" and "hold the wall!" as he attempted to shove a huge Q-tip up my tender bum, and twice I went sprawling.

You couldn't escape the clinic without a visit to the blood-draw table. As I turned away from the digging needle, the view through the windows—a dry little housing-project vegetable garden, traffic, and the distant houses of Potrero Hill—became for me the landscape of hope and regret: love, at any price.

In late 1978 I had signed the first of an endless series of release forms allowing several extra tubes of blood to be taken and tested for exposure to hepatitis B. That was the beginning of a new phase—the Hep Study—which at first coincided with my necessary check-ups and treatments for the clap but eventually became the sole purpose of my walks to Clementina.

My Clementina

Now I was summoned for blood-taking and injections of experimental hepatitis B vaccine (or, as it turned out, a placebo vaccine, and a year later, the real thing), and going to the clinic became a kind of public service. The people who drew my blood and took down my responses to the sex-contact and drug-use questionnaires were friendly, respectful, and grateful. I'd stroll back to work wounded but virtuous, a cotton ball taped to the crook of my arm. Thus was born my secret superstition: By taking part in the vaccine study, by letting my blood at appointed intervals, I staved off the Bad Thing. Syphilis, hepatitis, misfortune; I was as vague in my apprehensions then as a Transylvanian with a garlic necklace.

On my quarterly visits to the clinic, I saw my life quantified in the batteries of questions: *Was the number of partners with whom you had sex to orgasm since your last visit greater than ten? Number of times a partner ejaculated in your mouth? On average, of the three days a week on which you drank alcohol, how many drinks did you have?* Over time my answers went from belligerently high numbers to wistfully low.

Then the Hep Study was over and my visits to the clinic dwindled to nothing for a couple of years. During this time the Bad Thing took the very specific shape of the swelling AIDS mushroom cloud. Hunkered down, nobody I knew got VD anymore. When the HIV test debuted, I didn't rush out for it; I assumed I had been infected.

I heard about the AIDS death of an ex-boyfriend in October of '85, the night before I was to move in with my new lover, Jack. When he became ill six months later, we both got tested. We were positive, of course, and he was diagnosed with PCP. I didn't think much about my results, as I was otherwise healthy; all my attention was on Jack and his surviving.

A year later, someone from the clinic got in touch with me again—The Multi-City AIDS Cohort Study, or "MACS," it was now called, the strange statistical word *cohort* always suggesting *accomplice*, or more subliminally, *cavort*. Now I heard for the first time of that eerie vault of frozen blood samples at the CDC in Atlanta—row upon row of vials, like old bottles of poppers lodged in the back of the freezer, or ancestors in a family crypt, but only one date on each: *December 11, 1978; June 4, 1979; May 12, 1980; June 12, 1982; May 23, 1983.* I signed another release form and anti-body tests were run on an array of thawed-out samples of my blood, each further back in time. I imagined myself being siphoned into the past with every resuscitated teaspoon, becoming more transparent here in the present.

As with all the T-cell counts and viral-load results since, waiting for the next piece of information—when had I sero-converted?—was like being dangled over a bottomless pit and then yanked back onto firm ground.

"Some people don't want to know," I was warned.

"*I* do. When was it?"

"Your last negative result was June 12, 1982; the sample from May '83 tests positive."

That year, while still pining over Sam, I'd been having lots of what is now termed "unsafe sex" with: a blond dentist on vacation from his teaching post in Saudi Arabia who admired my straight teeth; a former high school tennis coach from Texas turned massage therapist I met sunbathing on the roof of Bonanza one lunch break; a darkly handsome French teacher from Boston University in town to visit an old friend dying from "that weird new gay cancer"; a hunky, closeted computer programmer with a stack of Koszinski novels beside his bed; a skinny, wild-eyed hairstylist who embarrassed me by yelling, "Give me all those little Kevins!" as I fucked him; my friends Michael, Gary, *and* Gina; and, on an unexpected layover, Steve, who was living with a lover in Monterey, but had come to the city on business.

Having accompanied Jack on so many lab visits, getting stuck was now freighted for me with the seriousness of a potentially terminal illness. They took larger amounts of blood when I went in, too—which took more time and a bigger needle—FedExing it off to half a dozen studies around the country. I climbed up on the paper-covered table and lay with my eyes shut.

There were still the sex questions, and the cigarette, alcohol, and pot queries, but things had taken a morbid turn, and sexual braggadocio gave way to the dementia parlor games of the neuropsych battery. I'd listen to a tediously detail-crammed story problem *(The cruise ship Regina left port on Tuesday, February twenty-two at three A.M. On the third day out, Anna Thompson, the cleaning lady, a redhead with bad dentures, had her purse stolen. She had six children, two of whom were undergoing expensive dermabrasion procedures...)* and then proudly recite back the torpid details. It was like having your gossip quotient measured.

A few days after a clinic visit, I'd get the call: "Your T-cells are 1,160" (or 1,210 or 1,050)—420-1250 was supposedly the normal range; below that you had to think about AZT or some anti-viral—and I'd go home to my dying lover who had ten, ashamed of my selfish elation at my good marks.

I cried during the blood draw the first time I went back after Jack died in June '88, suddenly too aware of having a

Kevin Bentley

body when he did not, certain grief had peeled my gripping fingers off the cliff edge of *nonprogression.* "I'm sorry," Dr. Buchbinder said. "Am I hurting you?"

Then I fell in love with Richard, who had to start AZT a few months after we met. I couldn't very well expect him to say "Hooray for you" when my numbers came back high every time and his steadily dwindled. He died three years later.

In the mid-nineties the study, relocated to plusher health-department offices on Van Ness (the old VD clinic at Clementina became for a time an art gallery), threw occasional "socials" at which researchers reported new information culled from participants' blood. Staring at images on a screen in a darkened room, I felt insubstantial as a ghost drifting through the data: the DNA bow ties, the pie charts, the ugly line graph whose bony arm rose ineluctably upward across the accumulating "years of infection" and the "numbers dead or diagnosed." We long-term nonprogressives crowd the center of our diminishing slice of the pie chart, scrambling as the music jerks to a halt and a few more chairs are gone.

In '97 I was informed that I carry the CCR5 mutation, one of two defective or variant genes that appear to delay the progression of HIV. At that time, of the 622 men whose blood samples have been tracked back to the early eighties, 12 percent remained long-term nonprogressives. More recently one study has identified a phenomenal HLA (human leukocyte antigen) type, with two alleles (alternative forms of genes) that are both protective against HIV progression on their own, and more so in the rare case of one individual having both. *B27* and *B57,* designations with appropriately military overtones—I have them both.

On a scale of one to ten, one being not very much, and ten *being a lot, which of the following do you feel is responsible for your continued good health?* * *Being a basically happy person (Three)* * *Spirituality (Zero)* * *Eating well and exercising regularly (Five)* * *Meditation and alternative therapies (Zero)* * *Having a living boyfriend (Ten).*

Three years after Richard died I met Paul, who charmingly misunderstood the discrete reference to "+nonprogressive" in my relationship ad and fell in love with me anyway when he learned his mistake. We've lived together very happily for eight years now, despite our so-called "discordance" (he's negative).

I go back to the MACS study (now the AIDS Office of the San Francisco Health Department) twice a year for blood to be drawn and shipped off to a series of studies—and to see if the sleeping giant has awakened and I'm to reckon with an infection that sometimes seems to me as historic as the Alamo. But my T-cells continue to range from 700 to 1,000. I'm no anti-treatment maverick—I'd take the drugs if I had to. It's hard not to assume I'll remain healthy when my counts remain stable after 21 years, though the noncommittal folks at the health department cheerfully tell me that today only 2 percent of the original study group remain nonprogressives. I still have to fight a gut fear (here comes that superstitious peasant) that if I talk too much about my good fortune, I'll be in for a rude surprise.

Without symptoms or daily pills, it's the blood draw that invariably highlights the fact I often allow myself to forget for days at a time, until I cut myself or the conversation comes round to retirement planning: I don't believe I'll get sick, but I can't depend on my good health. I stick out my arm, turn my head away and remember that housing-project garden and a vista promising the encircling arms of a lover, at the cost of a week's discomfort. The needle enters my vein and I'm adrift again, neither dead nor entirely among the living, lost in my heart's own current.

Widow-Hopper

I first saw the improbably named Willie Tedd when I walked in from work on a February evening in 1988 to find him sitting at the kitchen table eating lemon sorbet with my dying lover, Jack.

("Willie *Tedd?*" said my friend Louise at work the next day, aghast. "Doesn't he know the difference between a first and last name?"

"What about Brian Keith?" I said. "What about Billy Joel?"

"What about Hamburger *Mary?*" she snapped. "Get serious.")

I heard him first, actually, his giddy, high-pitched giggle followed by a lower-register admonishment to the dachshund, Henry, whose nails were clattering on the linoleum. Tall, with well-developed chest and arms and a small, unfinished-looking face (as if Gepetto had left off for lunch and never come back), he wore shiny black spandex bicycle shorts that bulged lewdly at the crotch, rubbery black Reeboks, a black T-shirt, and a shiny white plastic bicycle helmet that made him look as if he was about to climb into a cannon and be shot back to the Eagle. He didn't look much like a nurse. Or rather, he didn't look much like the other home-care help we'd had till now; Davies Medical Center, where Jack had just spent ten days, was crawling with snapping and camping male nurses who'd been very kind to us both.

I'd had a nerve-wracking hour earlier that day, waiting to hear if the caregiver agency could find a substitute for Gulima, the stolid but well-meaning Filipina who'd been spending weekdays with Jack for the last six weeks—after she'd taken sick and had to leave. Jack's condition had been changing at such a breakneck pace recently, I hardly recognized myself in the caregiver/administrator I'd become. When he came home from the first hospitalization, his condition had worsened drastically and his morphine dosage went up accordingly. I'd come home to find drawers upended on the floor, the mail unopened in the trash, and an empty saucepan on the stove, black and crackling over a flaming burner, Jack shuffling down the hall with huge dilated eyes, asking peevishly, "Are those three nuns in the living room coming with us on the tour bus?"

I made some desperate phone calls and filled out a lot of paperwork, and soon a home-care outfit in Daly City sent Gulima. Gulima wasn't unkind, but she was sealed off from us by her limited English and her practical dispassion, seemingly unfazed by the hothouse atmosphere of hysterical good cheer and white-knuckle skirmishes with death. Mostly she sat in the living room watching soaps and game shows and combing her lank hair, taking Jack's pulse and temperature now and then, and bringing him strictly measured doses of liquid morphine when he yelled.

I felt badly about going off to work and leaving Jack locked up all day like a toddler with a maid, but he insisted I stay on top of my job, and we couldn't afford for me not to. The surreal contrast of a brisk publishing office with the bubble bed, bedsores, oxygen tanks, and bottle of liquid morphine I had to hide in the kitchen cabinets behind cans of beef broth so Jack wouldn't overdose himself, accidentally or otherwise, made me wonder if I might be losing my grip. Taking care of Jack, I felt like Karen Black in *Airport* trying to keep that guy from getting sucked out the hole in the crashing plane. I tried calling Shanti, the volunteer organization that provided support for AIDS patients and their mates. They sent me Lewis, an overweight, depressed man whose main interest, once he heard I was in publishing, was in telling me the plot of his unfinished movie script about a gay *Love Boat*. He was clearly shocked by and afraid of Jack and he stayed as far from him as he could get. Between Jack's hard-fought eighty pounds and Lewis's bulk, it seemed as if we were all in one of those Woody Woodpecker cartoons where Walter Lantz's hand keeps reaching in and redrawing the characters in exaggerated ways.

"Have you talked to Jack about dying?" he'd ask, tucking into a big piece of chocolate cake at a nearby coffee shop. Jack, who was watching a lot of TV, was more interested in talking about Siskel and Ebert.

Talking to Lewis was supposed to make me feel better, but before long I found that avoiding a meeting with him cheered me up more. When I ended our relationship without closure, his parting shot was that I had a *lot* more grief work to do than I realized.

One day I came in from work and found Jack sprawled in an easy chair, urine-soaked, eyes rolled back in his head, Cheyne-Stoke breathing, Gulima boredly eating Ritz crackers from a greasy paper bag and watching *Wheel of Fortune.*

"Jack *tired,*" she said, glancing up at me. "He really snore." Five minutes later, for the second time in as many months, we were careening along in an ambulance, a couple of blasé paramedics shouting in Jack's face, "Mr. Sigesmund! Mr. Sigesmund! What day is it? Who's the president?" They shot him up with something that made his eyes roll right back into place and his mouth pop open like Charlie McCarthy's. "Friday, gentlemen. Reagan, unless somebody shot him while I was out."

So when Jack informed me that he and Willie Tedd had worked things out so that Gulima would be assigned to a new client and Willie would take over Jack's care, I could hardly protest.

"Who would you rather spend all day with?" Jack asked, chuckling.

Over the next four months Willie Tedd became a fixture in our lives. He and Jack hit it off so well, going out to movies and lunch when Jack was up to it; or watching videos and gorging the dog with jerky treats. Jack, sitting up in bed or lying on the couch, was like the urbane afternoon talk show host, Willie his laughing sidekick and sparring partner or charming guest, like Mike Douglas and Jaye P. Morgan.

Jack's old friend Charlie was a frequent guest, dropping over on his Tuesdays off to hang out and watch videos. On the phone one evening he asked, "Do you think Willie

Tedd's up to something with Jack?"

"C'mon!" I said. The handsome, vigorous, quick-witted man I loved had been worn down by opportunistic infections and grueling treatments for two years; the several hospitalizations the previous fall had reduced him to a frail, shuffling skeleton with huge, sunken eyes, who spoke and moved in slow motion. No, I didn't think he was having sex with Willie Tedd.

"Well, I'm just saying," Charlie said. "Willie Poppins sure is checking *you* out."

Willie *had* gotten a bit touchy-feely as time went on, bumping against me and hanging closely over my shoulder. He often arrived in the morning while I was in the shower or just stepping out, and several times he found reasons to pop into the bathroom. ("Jack needs his lotion!") And he gave me long hugs good-bye each time he left, but there was, after all, a lot of emotion in the air. I was grateful that he distracted and amused Jack. He wasn't someone I'd thought of sexually. The bulging muscles he labored at a Soloflex to swathe himself in seemed cosmetic; Willie, shrieking and swishing, was what Jack affectionately referred to as a Big Girl. The rolling pin he stowed in his spandex and 1977-vintage skin-tight Levi's seemed cartoonish, like a clown's inflated shoes, or a fool's scepter.

What kind of person has two first names? Looking at Jack's Week-at-a-Glance book one evening, which had once spilled over with doctor appointments, jotted blood-work results, and lists of new drugs he'd read about—now mostly blank unless I wrote something on it—an odd notation, almost haiku-shaped, caught my eye. In shaky, deteriorating block letters, he'd tried to write down Willie's name and phone number so he'd remember, garbling it several times, like someone trying to solve the Jumble: *wily deth.*

Jack came close to dying a week before his birthday in June—a small stroke or "episode," his doctor called it—then rallied for a bit, and we had a birthday dinner at a restaurant just around the corner from the apartment. The glittering yuppies' eyes glazed over when they saw Jack scuffing up to the table in his down house slippers and loose sweat suit, Willie and me each holding an arm. We had wine with dinner and Willie flirted with everyone and giggled more than usual. Back at the apartment, he lingered on the end of the bed till I yawned and reminded him how early I had to be up.

Jack opened his eyes for a moment when Willie had left. "He's got his eye on you—do you know that?"

I laughed. "He just wants another muscle queen in a leather vest!"

Jack died one morning not long after. Willie stole the show, sobbing hysterically, to the dismay of Jack's doctor, who needed his help with some necessary things. (Willie had bragged more than once that Dr. Jarvis had chased him around the apartment and grabbed his dick on his weekly visits. I'd hoped he was making it up.) The friends who'd rushed over to help were indignant at Willie's theatrics; he kept returning to the living room, only to run out again, sobbing. "D'you think *Willie Tedd*'s a stage name?" Louise said, handing me a cup of tea.

That night I went out to dinner in North Beach with a large group of Jack's and my friends. I'd invited Willie; it seemed awkward for him to just leave now that his official role was over. His grief in abeyance, he giggled shrilly and played footsie under the table, flushed with wine and, as he

Kevin Bentley

mentioned, an afternoon at the tanning salon.

I'd already had six months to mourn the loss of my lover; a large part of the person I'd known seemed to have rushed out along with the torrents of blood and vomit and worse in the hospital. After the jolt of the event itself, I went into a kind of zombie-like self-preservation mode: I rearranged the furniture, gave away Jack's clothes, bleached a streak in my hair, and changed my phone number after his mother, the Countess of Reno (Jack's stepfather had been a Spanish refugee "Count"), dried her tears and started calling up and leaving messages like, "Where's the *money?*" and "If a pair of brass elephant bookends are all he left his family, you can throw the ashes in the ocean for all I care!"

A week later, Willie Tedd rode his bike over to pick up a few items he'd left behind. I'd wanted to give him Jack's tux, which was much too big for me, and to thank him again for everything he'd done for Jack. When I walked him to the door, he turned and pasted his spandex-wrapped crotch against mine in an exploratory hug, and I knew, as I'd known on some level all along, that I could fuck him if I wanted to. He was an odd, effeminate muscle queen about whom I knew very little. We had nothing in common but Jack. Still, my body, reeling from two years of arm-wrestling death, decided for me. After a brief interlude of frantic grappling and flying clothing I was snapping on a Rough Rider and plowing Willie Tedd's Soloflexed butt with a zest that would have surprised me, had I been thinking. He was like a life-size inflatable doll, particularly in the glabrous, shaved area around his dick, which, in its superfluousness, was like a massive piece of Victorian furniture you have to keep stepping around. It was large and attractive, but seemed to serve no purpose. Slamming my cock in and out of his tightly gripping ass, I felt like I'd shot up from the bottom of some stifling deep and grappled onto his slick torso. I came with a shout, and saw Jack dead, beseeching arm outstretched, one eye staring open and the other crazily half-shut—("Can't you close his eyes?" I'd cried. "Do you have a little piece of Scotch tape?" Dr. Jarvis said.)

I figured Willie and I had better have a little talk.

"You know we've been thrust into intimacy by sort of dire circumstances—I mean, I don't think you'd look twice at me on the street or in a bar, right?" He grinned inscrutably at me with his small, carved-puppet features, but said nothing. "We both need some comfort right now, but I'm not sure where this can go. If this isn't enough for you, just say so and I'll understand." He rolled back onto his stomach and spread his muscular legs, burying his face in the strewn bed-covers, and the necessary discussion took a more urgent turn.

What I'd expected would be a one-time event occurred again a few days later, and then again, and after a couple of weeks I had to admit I was, what? dating? Willie Tedd. If my friends thought my fucking my dead lover's attendant unseemly, they were kind enough not to say so—though they weren't as tactful about the bleached streak. Willie had been assigned to a new case within days of Jack's death, and it was oddly comforting to hear him chatter about the new fellow and his lover and the difficulties they were having with the parents, who'd come to stay for the duration. Six years into the epidemic, Jack was the only sick person I knew, and I'd felt very alone. I needed to hear about others who were enduring what I had, needed to talk about Jack and shed all the exhausted, bitter, angry tears I'd been holding back, needed Willie's eager hug—and very much needed to strip off his skin-tight bicycle shorts or jeans, shove my aching boner up his clutching anus and fuck him till I squirted, sweat-drenched, panting, and trembling. I imagined that somehow Willie understood this purely physical and one-tracked connection and accepted it for what it was: we'd stared into the abyss of death together and like all healthy survivors who don't decide to become born-again Christians or Zen monks, we wanted to fuck our brains out while we were here, alive, and in possession of our uncorrupted flesh.

But I was wrong. Or, if he at first accepted the nature of our relationship, he changed in the weeks and then months that followed. It seemed to me I was no more Willie's type than he was mine—soon enough he'd tire of my boring, book-ish ways and dump me, and I'd say, "Gee, I'll miss you, but I understand." Instead, he kept coming back, but his behavior altered. I'd felt a protective fondness for the dizzy, giggling girlfriend in a gymbot's body; more often now I saw the flip side of that teenage girl—sulky, glowering. He'd come over and submit to being plowed—but afterward there was a dark atmosphere of resentment, as if I'd neglected to buy him flow-ers or deposit the folded currency on the nightstand. Had he imagined when Jack died he'd become mistress of Manderly? When we went out to eat he'd stare at his food and sulk.

I wasn't proud of the feeling, but the truth is that he embarrassed me in public. I felt like Mr. Belvedere escorting Mamie van Doren when we were out on the street together. Every walk to the corner with him was an adventure, because his tight duds, high-pitched laugh, and sashaying strut com-pelled a response, whether lewdly appreciative or homophobic, from passing traffic. His mannerisms had begun to grate: the flat, Midwestern twang; the way he said "Safeway's," instead of Safeway, "caraft," instead of carafe, and, often, "I just left that go in one ear and out the other."

I'd thought of Willie as a sort of blameless free spirit, à la *Nanny and the Professor,* but now I wasn't so sure. He seemed to have a lot of enemies we had to cross the road to avoid. ("Can't you just walk on by and ignore them?" I asked. "I would never be so *facetious!"* he snapped.) He confessed that his current roommate, an ex-lover, was evicting him, "for no reason at all."

"You've got so much extra room here," Willie said one evening, looking around my flat thoughtfully.

"Yes, but I have to move somewhere smaller I can afford right away," I said.

Now Willie wept. "I don't have enough cash to move!" And so I loaned him five hundred dollars of Jack's modest life insurance benefit.

One day I realized Willie hadn't mentioned his new client in a while. "I'm sick of talking about work," he said, when I asked. He was also tired of hearing about Jack—but then I could tell most of my friends were too. And I was changing. My thoughts had grown darker; some of the grief I thought I'd dealt with had only been put aside. Maybe Lewis was right about one thing: I had a lot more grieving to do than I'd understood. Sometimes I wondered how many people I'd had sex with were now dead. When I masturbated, I'd suddenly imagine them flitting around me like moths. I remembered reading a story once about sin-eaters, who come and eat food left out for the newly dead, ingesting their sins. How many newly grieving men had Willie Tedd fucked?

Kevin Bentley

While with me he sulked and clammed up, Willie was quite garrulous with Charlie, whom he'd taken to calling up to gossip about what a difficult boyfriend I was proving to be—and to drop hints about his desirability to others. Charlie would, naturally, repeat it all back to me in the most unflattering way.

"He's doing it with the lover—and this time the guy's not even dead yet."

"You mean—?"

"Yep—he's a professional widow-hopper."

Willie Tedd dropped by one evening soon after this, looking angry and grim, his thin lips pursed, as if he knew I'd unearthed his secret.

"This isn't working out," he said. "I just came by for my things." (There were extra pairs of spandex shorts tucked away here and there.) I tried to look suitably disappointed, but not too sad.

"I'm sure you're right. I'm so fucked up right now, it's not fair to you."

Jack's long decline had been the planet around which I revolved. Now everything was moving away from me at great speed, as if his death had shot a hole in the fuselage. Jack, Willie Tedd, the Countess: they moved in different directions, but they all moved away from me, Willie in a series of hang-up calls and slurry voice-mail messages, from terse ("Fuck you!") to bizarre ("We didn't discuss what to do about exchanging Christmas presents. Please let me know,") that only ended when I moved to a new apartment and changed my phone number once more.

Each night I climbed into bed like a space traveler slipping into his suspended-animation cylinder, knowing that one day, before I knew it, I'd be waking up lulled and unwrinkled to find it was a year later, Jack shrunk and flattened to a paper doll in a scrapbook.

Once I spotted Willie Tedd on the street—Glenn Close springing from the bathtub!—and he shouted a non sequitur ("Lick my asshole!") that turned a few heads. Then he sank for the last time into that same blissful black hole of forgetfulness that swallowed up all of the worst of that time—Jack's vile mother, the snotty German woman upstairs who rode her Exercycle noisily over our bedroom right through the very moment Jack expired, insurance forms, condom catheters, hospice pamphlets on *How to Let Go*.

Let's Shut Out
the World

For three years I spent nearly every Sunday treasure-hunting out at H. Drew Crosby's brown-shingled Edwardian house at Seventh and Lake in San Francisco's Richmond District alongside my lover, Richard. In the first weeks he and I got to know each other, Richard had told me so much about Drew that she seemed to me like someone I'd read about in a book before I actually met her, and she *was* a character and had been all her life, from the time her father gave her the pair of sailor pants she'd demanded for her birthday at ten, which she promptly wore to church with a World War I trench helmet. (The following Sunday the priest decried "the girl who wears sailor pants—and you all know who I mean!")

Her partner of fifty-five years, Marian Pietch, had just died, and Drew had decided she wanted to sort out and sell most of the dusty books, antiques, and junk that sandbagged the creaking old house from top to bottom, instead of leaving it all to be carted away at her own death. She loathed the idea of some sharp-eyed dealer coming in and cherry-picking the most valuable items, but Richard also thought she was ashamed when she imagined strangers seeing just what a mess Marian's and her home had become. They hadn't cleaned in twenty-five years, too feeble to do it themselves and too suspicious to let a maid in. It wasn't unusual chez Drew to come across the abandoned remnants of a decade-old cup of coffee and bread crust on a shelf; or a petrified dog turd behind a stack of moldering books, evidence of Lillie, a Dalmatian they'd owned in the sixties, named for Lillie Coit (the fire truck chaser whose bequest built Coit Tower), and famous for having eaten a first edition of George Moore's *Esther Waters* and Marian's wristwatch.

Richard had known Drew and Marian for ten years before he was allowed to set foot inside their house. They'd bought the 1902 two-flat building from the original owner around 1940. He had never rented the downstairs unit and neither did they; instead the two women filled it up with the books, antiques, and ephemera they obsessively collected. In the beginning the upstairs flat, where they lived, was nicely decorated with antiques, art, and oriental carpets on the wood floors, books properly relegated to the many cases in every room; by the time Richard first saw it, they could barely get to the kitchen or bathroom without falling over the toppling stacks of books and papers filling the floor and piled up and down either side of the long hall and the stairs.

As a young woman Marian had worked for famous bookseller and *Chicago Tribune* critic Fanny Butcher in Chicago, and she began amassing books early. I have a worn little leather-bound edition of *Vanity Fair*, between the pages of which are pressed fragile four-leaf clovers, ferns, and flower petals; lightly penciled on the flyleaf: *Marian Meyer, Chicago 1920,* and in a later hand, the letters *NFS* (not for sale).

Marian had been the real reader. Drew, like Richard, liked to pull some quirky old title from the shelf and browse around in it. Drew liked Irish folktales and history. She had particularly collected editions of Gertrude Stein and George Moore, though she didn't pretend to read either. (If her photo was being taken, Drew liked to assume what she called her "Gertrude pose," leaning forward in her chair with one hand on her thigh, the other extended slightly, as in the Picasso portrait.) When Richard wasn't reading auction catalogs for the children's books he collected—early editions of Lewis Carroll, series like *Goops, Uncle Wiggily,* and the *Oz* adventures—he read whatever had caught his eye on the way out the door past the bookcase-lined walls in his house on Elgin Park. Two nights before he went to the hospital he left on the floor beside my bed a first edition of *The Witch of Wall Street, Hetty Green,* the biography of a notoriously stingy millionaire.

Once Marian and Drew were established on Seventh Avenue, they began acquiring in earnest: when the unfortunate Japanese were being hustled off to internment camps, Drew and Marian were there to pick over and cart home items from the hastily abandoned belongings on the sidewalks of the Fillmore. Twenty-five years later, when an ill advised urban-renewal plan demolished block after block of sagging Victorians and scattered their black inhabitants, they bargained for the disgorged contents. When someone in an immigrant Chinese family died and, by custom, his belongings were all gathered up in a sheet and taken to the city dump, Drew and Marian followed them and rifled the deceased's effects, returning home with jewelry, fine silk pajamas, and, once, a set of false teeth, which they passed along to a toothless man they met on a bus. They referred to the dump as "the garden" in conversation, so people wouldn't know where they'd been. When Laurel Hill Cemetery was dismantled and built over, they lugged home a couple of slim pioneer tombstones and propped them against the wall in their basement, where they gathered cobwebs.

Once a week through the forties and fifties, they drove to the Masonic Street mansion of a crippled, elderly bachelor named Alexander Leonard to hear his tales of nineteenth-century San Francisco and purchase books, paper, photos, and furniture from his collection. Their taste was both eclectic and specific: a deep closet beneath the stairs in the lower flat held ornate carved boxes of tarnished Victorian silverware; sweet-smelling waist-high stacks of brittle 78 rpm "race records"; a metal chest full of battered daguerreotypes and ambrotypes packed in yellowed tissue; a fat velvet photo album full of cabinet-card photos of circus performers and freaks; a stiff leather doctor's bag filled with surgical tools and vials of liquids and powders that had belonged to Leonard's father, a physician. A corner cupboard nearby, its glass almost opaque with cobwebs, held dozens of staring porcelain doll heads, like Princess Langwidere's cabinet of spare heads in *Ozma of Oz*. They had collected old dolls for years; at one time as many as five hundred stared from within glass cases or perched on shelves around the rooms, till one day Marian said she couldn't bear them looking at her anymore, and they sold most of them off. I loved imagining her and Drew with their fancy-dressed Victorian lady dolls with pearl earrings and their Dutch-boy, sailor, and Shirley Temple dolls. Did they rearrange them, name them, play with them? "Don't be *cute*," Drew said sourly when I asked.

I met Richard fifteen months after Jack died. The bar forays I'd made quickly confirmed that I wasn't going to be finding my next boyfriend sitting in the shoeshine chair at the Jackhammer or leaning into the chain-link fence that ran down the middle of the Detour; the scene was still very much decimated by AIDS in '89, and at thirty-three, I'd left behind the hectic, beer-slugging, bong-smoking bad boy of pre-'85. I'd been yanked off the party by the seriousness of Jack's pneumocystis diagnosis scarcely six months after we'd moved in together. It had been him and me against the world, and when he was gone I was left with some good furniture, a miniature dachshund named Henry, a yawning silence, and, somewhat guiltily at first, an unfamiliar, calm gratitude for my life, which, despite grief and loneliness, seemed blessed after long months of sickbed, horror, and hospital.

My best friend, Bob, had recently taught me to play rac-quetball, and one evening Richard, a casual acquaintance of his who sometimes stopped in Bob's shop, The Magazine, came along. After several of these sporty meetings at the Tenderloin Y, including discreet appraisals while changing and showering in the Y's grimy locker room, and congenial dinners during which Richard's leg pressed against mine beneath the table, I quizzed Bob. "I think you can have an affair with him if you let him know that you're interested— but just remember, he's married." When Richard offered to drive me home one night, well before we reached my Noe Street basement flat where Henry waited yapping at the door, we'd established that we were both very interested, that we were both positive but so far healthy, and that one of us, at least, was sure that his longtime partnership with another man, which had ceased to be sexual or romantic years before, was no impediment. He'd gotten sober after typically rambunctious twenties and thirties and the loss of many acquaintances to AIDS, including his closest friend who'd moved out from Kentucky with him, and he hadn't had sex in the several years since becoming Richard *H.* He owned and ran Fields, a quaint old Polk Street metaphysical bookstore, in partnership with an egocentric, tactless, ninety-seven-year-old follower of the late mystic Gurdjieff. His bookish intelligence, self-deprecating wit, hesitant Kentucky accent and essential kindness all attracted me to him before I had a clear take on what we might do when we were finally alone and naked.

We sat on the couch talking for an hour, then fell silent and looked at each other. "Could I kiss you?" he said. A little later we pushed apart, wrestled out of our clothes, and sat back for a moment, panting and hard, staring again. I hadn't had sex in a year, not since Willie. He grinned and, reaching for me, said, "I'm going to eat you alive."

Like us, Drew was recently bereaved, fairly certain her turn wasn't far off, glad for the present but half-living in the past and in love with relics. I dreamt about her before I met her. I was leaving her house, without Richard for some reason, and as soon as she pulled the door shut behind me I heard her say, "I *wish* you could see Marian—she's here now." My feet, of course, were frozen in place. I knew Marian was standing on the other side of the door. Why should she terrify me so? I woke myself up yelling *please stop you're scaring me.*

Kevin Bentley

"You look like you've seen a ghost," Drew said, skewering me with a gimlet-eyed look that would become familiar. This was my first visit—only days after Richard and I had first slept together—and I'd been staring at her since she opened the front door and rusty security gate with several of the jailor's wad of keys that hung from a ring on her pocket and shambled ahead of us up the dark-green-painted steps, past the peeling thirties-era cabbage-rose wallpaper, to the wreck of a kitchen at the far end of the dust- and mildew-smelling upstairs flat, her giant ass stretching a lifeless pair of black polyester men's slacks. Richard had brought her the hamburger she'd craved, and she sat in a metal folding chair at the fifties dinette table taking large bites, chewing, and blinking slowly. She was massive, her large hanging breasts dammed at her wide waist by the tightly belted slacks. She didn't exactly seem like a "fat lady"; she was egg-shaped, with dainty little feet in a pair of men's black leather shoes—in fact, she was dressed entirely in men's clothing. Later, Richard would open her bedroom closet door and show me the hangers full of identical black slacks and belts, white dress shirts, and rows of polished black shoes. But I was mesmerized by her face. It was pale white, heavily scored with wrinkles and spattered with angry red blotches like an old sea captain's. Her eyebrows and lashes, like her short-cropped hair, were a yellowed gray, which gave her red-rimmed eyes an albino look. One eye welled with something slightly more viscous than tears, which occasionally brimmed up enough to roll down her face, at which point she wiped it with the back of her sleeve. "What is this, feeding time at the monkey cage?" she said, and then laughed her phlegmy Popeye laugh, *kekekekekek*, showing horsey yellow dentures, half-chewed hamburger, and a surprisingly red tongue. She reminded me of the zoo gorilla who looks

145

at you petulantly out of the corner of his eye as if to say *don't you see I'm as human as you?* but might at any moment shriek and rush the bars. Her rough features conjured racist old *Punch* caricatures I'd seen that depicted the Irish as coarse-faced simians. Her yellowed white Buster Brown hairdo and girth faintly recalled *Captain Kangaroo* creator Bob Keeshan—but the similarity ended there.

After high school, where she'd been a notorious tomboy, Drew enrolled in a Manhattan nursing school run by nuns, but she was caught having sex with a senior by Sister Ursula one night in the dorm, and her parents were summoned by telegram to retrieve her, as were the parents of all six girls Drew had slept with. Drew had already made inquiries and discovered another, Jewish run nursing school, attached to Newark's Beth Israel Hospital. "Kick me out, I don't care," she said, laughing in the faces of the shocked nuns, "the *Jews* will take me."

Her parents took her to a Jesuit, Father Rudke, for counseling, and she told him her whole history. "You are the most honest person I've ever met," he said. To her father, he confided that "it's much harder to straighten out women than men." Then her father took her to a doctor in Newark who diagnosed her abnormality as a congested uterus and treated her for a time with mild shocks from a sort of electric garter belt. "I wasn't aware of any distress," Drew would say, chuckling.

Early in the Depression she left school and hitchhiked around the country dressed as a boy. Landing in Chicago and out of work, she bought a black dress and heels and took a job as a B-girl in a dance club called Agnes's Club Era, where she began a tempestuous relationship with a fellow dancer called Peg; their song was "These Foolish Things." Drew was too husky and clumsy to stick with tea-dancing for long, and in 1934 her parents paid for her to finish nursing school in Chicago.

One night in a bar she met a pretty, slender older woman with sharp features, bee-stung lips, and long brown braids coiled on either side of her delicate head. Marian was camping out at some women friends' apartment and claimed she didn't know how to open the roll-away bed; Drew offered to come over and help. They spent the night together, and in the morning Drew brought Marian coffee in bed and crouched behind her to brush her uncoiled hair while she sat up sipping it, naked. Later that day, Drew dumped Peg; Marian, who'd been married for ten years to an insurance man named Pietch, never went home again, and some months later Mr. Pietch shot himself. One Sunday afternoon, in the bottom of a crate from which I'd been pulling old porcelain doll limbs wrapped in crumbling newspaper, I found a deco-framed black-and-white studio portrait of a middle-aged man reminiscent of Clifton Webb, along with a 1935 date book filled with neatly noted business appointments, a brittle clipping with the headline *Chicago Man Found Shot to Death* tucked inside. *"Put that back,"* Drew snapped when I held the photo up quizzically.

Richard's house, though regularly cleaned, wasn't so different from Drew's. Both were cool, dark, mildewed, and reeked of old books. The low arched doorway on Elgin Park was like a hobbit hole, and inside, closely packed bookcases rose up twelve feet on either side of the long, wide hallway, with old framed prints and portraits hanging askew across them and chandeliers and old chairs dangling from the ceiling, Alice's tunnel made horizontal. The main living space, beyond a mirrored door at the other end, was open and gutted, with bare rafters high above, partially Sheetrocked walls lined with old bookcases and further up, several tinted, framed, panoramic Yosemite photos, oriental carpets spread around a scarred softwood floor, and a huge stone hearth taking up much of one wall—according to city records, the downstairs had been a blacksmith's shop. Upstairs was a small Victorian flat Richard and his partner rented out.

When I had first arrived in San Francisco a dozen years before, the air and light were jarringly new to me—the cool, slightly misting or foggy mornings and evenings, the comforting aroma of damp old wooden houses. I'd never seen Victorians before and felt as if I were on a movie back lot as I wandered down gingerbread blocks in the Castro, staring at yellow-lit windows and tiny front yards behind low wrought-iron fences, as laughter and music drifted out. From Hackney Brothers, the hundred-year-old family dry-goods store Richard wandered as a child back in London, Kentucky, with its creaking wood floor and attic full of ancient mannequins and out-of-date merchandise, to his bookstore, Fields, with all its original 1932 fixtures down to the delicate, round-based black telephone and clacking, monstrous Remington typewriter, to the house on Elgin Park—Richard lived inside this same dusty black-and-white photograph I'd wanted to enter since I was a boy daydreaming over *Gone-Away Lake* and *Mystery of the Moss-Covered Mansion*.

In the spring of 1939 Marian and Drew left Chicago in a '33 Auburn and drove cross-country, stopping in Texas to buy a cowboy hat and boots for Drew and an oversized sombrero for Marian, and photographing each other in their Western getups at Carlsbad Caverns in New Mexico. In these snapshots, which hung framed at the end of the dark upstairs hall, Drew looks like a grinning, husky boy. Marian, in an embroidered peasant blouse and jodhpurs, lips pursed, aims a toy pistol at the camera in imitation of the famous Bonnie and Clyde images.

When they reached San Francisco they drove straight to Mona's 440, the North Beach lesbian club they'd heard about in Chicago. It was still daylight, and they sat in the car with the motor running, debating whether to go in, till a business-suited man with a pen and notepad squinted at their license plate, and Drew threw the car into gear and they lurched away.

They took civil service exams and got jobs as police matrons. The cops called Marian "Biscuits" because of her Princess Leia-like coils of hair. They were lesbians of the old order—that is, with good reason, they were paranoid and stubbornly ambiguous about being labeled gay, suspicious of strangers, and difficult to approach. Though she lived most of her life in physical intimacy with another woman, and gathered a huge collection of books and ephemera by or about literary lesbians and gay men, Marian would adamantly proclaim, "Don't lump me in with *Them!*"—meaning The Lesbians. After Marian took an early disability retirement—a prostitute had kicked her in the knee during a strip search—they were certain they'd been put under surveillance and swore they'd spotted camera-wielding detectives peering through the back fence to see if they could catch Marian doing cartwheels, or, presumably, exhibiting sapphism. On an increasingly well-to-do block of spacious, upper-income homes, they put up chain-link fence and a barred entry gate, to the consternation of their bridge-playing Junior League neighbors. They installed wooden shutters on the windows and every evening, Marian would sweep them all closed and announce, "Let's shut out the world."

Within months of our meeting, Richard's blood work showed falling T-cells and his HMO doctor put him on a high dosage of AZT. He quickly became unwell and anemic. Our sex had been more romantic than lustful from the start. Kissing, holding each other as we slept, happiest in each other's company: still reeling from Jack's death and now starting down the same path with Richard, this devotion was all that I wanted or needed. Sex was heavy petting; we necked as he jerked me off. "Mine's broken," he'd say if I reached for his dick. Once, much later on, when I insisted he go further—Didn't sex fix everything?—he let himself be aroused and brought to orgasm, but the come that pooled on his stomach had a sort of rust in it he took for blood. "See what I mean?" he said, shaking his head. "Broken."

The women had nothing to do with their families after they left Chicago, except for a brief interval when Drew's mother followed them to California and tried to live with them, but she and Marian fought bitterly. "That woman looks like a broken-down Chinese whore," she said of Marian (was she wearing those silk pajamas? I wondered), and so Drew asked her to leave, and though she remained in the same city, they never saw her again. Drew was putting her key in the gate one day twenty years later when a neighbor yelled, "Oh my

God, I thought you were dead!" This woman had seen an obituary in the paper for "Helen Crosby"—Drew was Helen Drew Crosby, but she never used her given name—but it was actually Drew's mother who'd died, and that was how she found out about it.

Marian bought The Lion Bookshop from its elderly owner, who had decided to retire, and moved it to a storefront on Polk Street. This was around the same time that Richard first came to work a few doors down, at Fields, in the early seventies. Marian liked reading, collecting, and researching the value of books, but not selling them. Most of her stock was marked *NFS* inside the front cover. The Lion was the kind of dusty little shop you can never seem to find open, but if you put your nose to the dirty window you might see a mean-looking elderly lady in a beret poring over an auction catalog beside a pile of books; if you tapped on the glass, she'd mouth "Go away."

Richard had slowly become friends with Marian over the years; sometimes she'd even sell him a book. When Marian closed her store, after a decade or so, he helped her pack up and bring all her books home. He would go out to meet her once a week for coffee and pastries at a bakery near their home and talk books. It was Richard the elderly women called to drive them to the emergency room when one got sick. Marian, in her nineties, grew ill, frail, and blind. Drew, always a big-boned girl and now obese in her seventies, couldn't care for her. Drew summoned Richard late one night, and led him up the stairs and down the hall to their cluttered bedroom where Marian lay, drenched and shivering with fever. She pulled back the covers and lifted one of Marian's breasts to show him the angry rash beneath it. Soon after that, Marian went to live for a short, sad time at Hillhaven, a nursing home less than a mile away. She called it *Hellhaven*. Her mustache grew in, upsetting her, though she couldn't see it herself. Richard went out and bought an electric razor and shaved her.

She'd had to be hospitalized by the time I met Richard, and she died a few weeks later. Marian had made Richard the executor of her will, which left everything to Drew, and both their wills otherwise left the estate to Guide Dogs for the Blind. She had depended on him to help Drew cope when she died, and he took pains to see that Drew's affairs were in order, her bills and taxes were paid, and she had food in the fridge.

Though he was courtly and charming with people in general and endlessly patient with the croaking nonagenarian witch Ruth Cooke, with whom he owned the bookstore, and the stream of simple-minded or obsessed New Agers, pagans, and secretive Gurdjieffian customers, Richard was privately a gleeful mimic. He imitated Ruth's boasting of shopping for boots ("And the girl said to me, 'You've got the legs of a sixty year old!'") or her staggering out of the stock room with a mustache of crumbs from the feta cheese she'd been wolfing from a paper bag, her chin sawing the air like Hepburn's, shrieking, "That Negro took my *purse!*" When customers' farts reached the cash register, he'd wail, "Shoooo-*eeee!*" and light a stick of incense. In the Safeway checkout line behind a Polk Street denizen with a dozen flat, greasy strands of hair in a lifeless ponytail and a bottle of gin on the counter, he'd whisper in my ear, "*Alcoholic hair.*" Recounting some windy anecdote from a customer, he'd put one hand on his hip and assume a shocked matron's voice: "And *then* she said…" He liked to make inanimate objects greet me warmly, from a baby doll in a dime store to a fresh Malbeck in its shell at Anchor Oyster Bar, whose lips he manipulated with a toothpick to make it squeak "Hi, Kevvie!" Like Gillian humming to Pyewacket in *Bell, Book and Candle,* he had a little tune he'd sing to his cat, Smokey, while it "made bread," kneading its claws on his chest.

Though we saw each other every day, he regularly mailed me postcards, the message usually typed in the jumpy, ink-clogged letters of the store's ancient Remington. They were almost always old: cartoon dachshunds delivering German punch lines, Louis Wain cats in short pants having a pie fight, the interior of Rick's Speakeasy Lounge in some fifties motel, a witch whizzing over a row of Model T's in downtown Salem. A postcard with a black-and-white photo of a large black woman in a muumuu reaching to stick a bill in the G-string of a glistening muscleman read: *Oh honey! Just a quick note to let you know that his eye is still on the sparrow—like her eye is on the lizard.*

Drew fell ill with pneumonia after Marian died and almost died in the hospital herself, but then she rallied and came home again. Because of things she'd seen in her brief nursing stint in the thirties, she didn't trust hospitals, and while she was hospitalized she'd paid for a private nurse to stay by her side through the nights. This woman, Lois, a slovenly, sixty-ish Catholic crackpot with gray, alcoholic hair, did her best to scare Drew into returning to her childhood Catholicism. She bragged about secret missions she'd undertaken for the pope and bullied Drew, who'd worn men's clothes since she was a teenager, into wearing tacky beaded sweaters and other more gender-"appropriate" clothing that, ironically, did make her look like a cross-dresser. She nagged Drew about having Marian's ashes in the house, claiming to detect mysterious wafts of incense in the hall when she visited, a sign of some busybody saint's disapproval of unconsecrated remains. As if she were selling Drew a car, the two of them haggled endlessly over what it would cost to posthumously convert and have masses said for Marian, a bitter atheist. Drew and Marian had carted home some religious icons over the years, including a couple of nasty-looking wax Madonnas, historic objects looted in Europe during World War II that they'd found in pawnshops and flea markets. Lois talked her into taking all that over to the Little Sisters of the Revolving Door, as Richard referred to the convent a few blocks away, since the nuns were sequestered and Drew would have to place her offerings in a screened lazy Susan affair where they'd be swept away by little snub-nailed, liver-spotted hands with a lisped "Bless you."

Then, happily, as Drew's health got better, she had a falling out with Lois, who Drew claimed had billed her for every tête-à-tête, and we heard no more about her for a time.

Unless we were out of town—and before Richard's health worsened or between bouts of pneumocystis, we made trips to Amsterdam, Paris, London, Santa Fe, and Key West—we almost always drove out to Drew's on Sunday morning, stopping on the way to pick up pastries or sandwiches. After drinking strong tea, eating, and catching up on her news at the kitchen table, we'd troop down the hall to one of the jammed rooms, or downstairs to the lower flat, or to the basement. Drew would sit on a low stool with an open box or pile of books before her, picking up whatever caught her fancy and reeling out stories we might or might not have heard before. Richard always said she looked like an elephant eating peanuts as the cascading mound of cast-aside papers, photos, and books rose around her.

There were junk books like, say, a badly sunned volume two of *The Tontine* or a book-club edition of *King of the Castle* by Victoria Holt, which went to Friends of the Library in box after box; obviously valuable books we gathered by subject and carted to California Book Auction, from whom Drew periodically received large checks. There was an amazing Henry Miller collection of signed firsts and photos, since she and Marian had owned a little cottage in Carmel where they'd spent a lot of time in the fifties. We pulled from a closet a sheet-wrapped impressionistic painting of Drew sitting naked beside a mineral bath at Big Sur playing a recorder, and we hung it over the fireplace in her sitting room.

Hours would pass while we dug and reached and coughed in the raised dust, our skin coated with it; each of us eventually collapsing onto a chair or rug with a book or pile of papers that had finally absorbed us. One Sunday I cut open a carton bound with yellowed tape to find a trove of mint-condition lesbian pulps. Drew feigned surprise. "Get those out of here," she said. I pictured the prim Marian with her coiled braids and beret nervously buying them one at a time at some newsstand, reading those *frank portrayals of a twilight world* behind closed doors, and then secreting them away.

Richard usually filled a box with books he was interested in, and at the end of the day, we'd go though them—and whatever I'd tossed in—with Drew and she'd name a price, and Richard would write her a check. I liked the obscure gay literary fiction, biographies, and autobiographies—an early edition of Lord Alfred Douglas's self-serving autobiography, a water-stained Hogarth Press edition of *Mr. Norris Changes Trains*, several volumes of Beaton's diaries—and the odd titles, like a Grabhorn Press Poe bibliography; a pretty 1907 copy of Mary Wilkins's ghost stories, *The Wind in the Rose-Bush;* or a bizarre 1943 beauty book by movie star Joan Bennett, *How to Be Attractive*. One afternoon, pulling a photo- and paper-stuffed bureau away from the peeling wall, I exposed a dozen dust-caked baseballs beneath it, and called Drew over to see. "That was Marian," she said sheepishly. "She hated those kids hitting their balls into the yard." Another time I was admiring a worn old Windsor chair that sat in the unused bathtub in the lower flat, stacked with sheets and towels, when Drew said, "You like it? That's a good chair. You can have it for a hundred."

"Wow," Richard said later on the drive home. "She likes you—that was Marian's chair behind her desk at The Lion."

When the light was fading at the windows, we'd wash up, brew more tea, and sit with Drew in her cluttered, artifact-strewn kitchen or back parlor, eating cookies and drinking from mismatched old china cups, while she talked about the past. She remembered and could describe events of many decades before down to the last detail—for instance, the people who picked her up and the places she went when she hitchhiked around the country as a girl, the seesaws on the rooftop of the mental hospital she worked at in Chicago and the laundry chutes between floors she and the other young attendants slid down; the carousing she'd done with several women pals in the fifties, till Marian put her foot down. "Oh life begins at forty, believe me," she liked to say, chuckling, but this wasn't at all true for Richard, whose life was draining away at forty-two.

As he stacked books and blew the dust from fragile sheet music and loose engravings, I saw but refused to register Richard's body being siphoned away, pared in subtle increments, his face becoming drawn, his cornflower-blue eyes anxious and tired looking behind the wire rim glasses. While he pored over issues of *The Bookman* and sent away for first editions of *Oz* and *Uncle Wiggily* volumes, his blood thinned with anemia, the hair on his head turned dull and feathery as a baby's from the severe pneumocystis treatments, and the blond hair on his chest and legs disappeared. How well could Drew see? Sometimes I thought I saw her eyeing him shrewdly.

While Drew could be surprisingly informed and up to date on some topics, she was ignorant and superstitious about illness. Richard had warned me all along that Drew wouldn't react well if he talked to her about the virus. He knew she and Marian had had close friends over the years they'd abruptly turned against and never spoken to again. "'Talk to my lawyer,' I told him," she'd say of someone she'd cut off. She told us once how her old Chicago lover, Peg, showed up in San Francisco years later and wanted to visit, but Marian was jealous and forbade it. Then, years after that, Drew heard that Peg was dying of cancer, but Marian still wouldn't let her see her. "A cigarette that bears a lipstick's traces...," she'd warble hoarsely when she told this story, and mop her eyes with her sleeve. Once, after a doctor's appointment, she said, "I'm afraid of ending up a helpless invalid, all by myself!" and began to sob with her red face in her hands and her nose running, like a giant child.

"We'll look out for you, Drew, don't you be silly,"

Richard said, his hand on her shoulder—believing it, I think.

The idea had always been to make Drew's house livable again, and to make room for her to live with and enjoy her nicest things. Sending books to auction, lugging boxes and furniture to the basement, and throwing a yard sale one weekend—at which her frankly curious but wary neighbors browsed and craned their necks for a glimpse inside the open front door, and a middle-aged man, a neighbor's grown son, reclaimed a few baseballs—we cleared the lower flat for cleaning and painting, then arranged furniture, rugs, and clocks, and hung photos and paintings, and Drew, her elderly parrot Alberta, and the pound mutt she'd recently adopted, moved down.

"Marian was here again last night," she'd often say as we arrived at the door, looking sidelong at us to judge our reaction. She claimed to regularly wake up in the night and see Marian coming down the hall with Lillie.

Drew's backyard, with a stately fir in the far corner that towered over the house, looked directly into Mountain Lake Park, which gave the back rooms the aura of being in the country. Marian had once kept a lush garden, but by the era of our visits it was long since overgrown with vines and weeds. One autumn I waded down into it with several large bags of daffodil bulbs and dug holes and planted them randomly, while Drew and Richard sorted books upstairs. The following March Drew phoned us on a Sunday morning crowing "*Darling Kevin and Richard!*"—the view from her rickety back deck a sea of daffodils.

Around November of 1992, Richard's health started failing. The HMO doctor first misdiagnosed his third bout of pneumocystis as TB. Anyone who'd been in close proximity to him, we were told, should get a chest X ray, so he had to tell Drew to get one, with much misgiving. It turned out not to be TB, but by then the damage was done. While we logged another ten days of grim visits to the infusion clinic, Drew took up with Lois again. Her health was generally good, but Drew was obese, slightly diabetic, and eighty-one years old. She'd recently gotten herself one of those MedicAlert contraptions to wear around her neck, with a button she could press for help if she fell down. Naturally, Drew frequently cried wolf, pressing the button "accidentally," which meant Richard would get a call from the MedicAlert people if they couldn't reach her by phone, and he'd have to drive over to check on her.

We didn't see her for several Sundays after the TB scare. Then one day in late November Richard got a MedicAlert call—Drew had hit the button. When he tried calling to check on her he got no answer, so he raced over. No answer at the door, only Alberta screeching from the back of the house. He tried to put his key in the gate and it no longer fit—she'd changed the locks. He knew then, but he walked around the corner and looked for her in the park anyway. He found her shambling along the sidewalk with her dog, Maxie. She wouldn't speak to him or meet his eyes. "What's the matter, Drew? What's wrong?"

"Talk to my lawyer," she said, turning away.

After that she refused to open the door to him or talk on the phone. Of course Lois had told her the only people who were getting TB nowadays were people with AIDS.

That evening Richard walked into my apartment to tell me what had happened, and as he stood there with Henry jumping at his legs and yipping, he burst into tears and sobbed inconsolably for the first time since I'd known him.

"I *knew* this would happen if she found out! I *knew* it!" I held him and stroked his head. "It doesn't matter. You knew how she was. It doesn't matter." But it did. In mid-December he came down with PCP again, went to the hospital with a collapsed lung, and died a week later. Why, I wondered, did her betrayal do him more harm than my love did good?

Word of her drifted back to me periodically over the next several years. Somebody reported that she'd let some Irish immigrants move into the top flat. She was bedridden, it was said, and attended fulltime by a nurse—Lois? Then a friend called to tell me he'd seen an ad in the paper for a garage sale at Drew's address, so he went. While strangers milled around in the musty basement picking over the items for sale, an elderly woman wailed deliriously upstairs.

I wasn't yet living with Paul, but we were spending most nights together at my apartment or his loft by December '97. Over dinner on New Year's Eve, he asked me to move in and we set a date. It was cold and wet, and by the time we crawled into bed it had begun to rain hard, wind rattling the eighteen-foot windows and tearing at the skylights. I noticed in the *Chronicle* obituaries the following week that Drew had died that night, at eighty-five. I wondered what smart baby dyke would retrieve those prized Carlsbad snaps from the thrift store or dumpster and hang them on her wall as quaint, anonymous proto-lesbians.

Random events in those first days after Richard's death had seemed significant, valedictory—Henry leaping from the couch and wagging his tail at nothing, a lamp switching itself on or off or the bulb blowing, power outages extending no further than my one-block street. The week before he died, Richard had apparently sent off a check for two nineteenth-century gold coins, and they duly arrived two weeks after he was cremated and his ashes placed in a hollow leather volume his roommate had a bookbinder make with his name and dates on the spine. *Richard: The Book*, his brother back in Kentucky dubbed it.

The book closed half-read, the shutters snapped shut; the house on Seventh was gutted and sold. Tea parties at the monkey cage; Drew waving from her doorway as we drove away— "I won't be able to sleep for thinking of you two!"; lying in bed with Richard as he sighed and put aside his book and kissed the side of my head: no artifact can bring that back.

Chimayó

The summer before Richard's death we traveled to Santa Fe because I wanted to show him the sky—and the famously clear high-altitude light that razored the red hills, hunter-green clusters of juniper, and buttery light-brown Flintstone adobes so sharply into focus. As if that 7,000-feet-above-sea-level clarity could restore the blurring edges of his advancing illness. And we came at the urging of the retired movie star acquaintance I'd gotten to know when I edited her memoir. The book was too much spiritual regeneration and too little Hollywood scoop to sell, but I had loved rooting through the cardboard carton of jumbled snapshots, studio stills, and lobby cards she sent for the photo insert, and hearing her unmistakable rushed, creamy voice over the phone, the same voice that had brushed off Sinatra's smutty flirtations to chide him about his unfinished novel. A cool, intelligent blonde, Martha most often played the rueful girlfriend who knew that Bill or Cary really loved Audrey or Sophia. She was charmed by Richard's London, Kentucky courtliness, and forgave his innocently asking if she'd known Chaplin. ("He was a *little* before my time, dear.")

Martha had insisted we visit Chimayó—El Santuario de Chimayó, the Lourdes of America, thirty miles outside of Santa Fe—and she came to pick us up armed not with candles or head scarf, but an old tablespoon and a pink plastic grocery bag. We were going for the miracle dirt. "I use it for my hands, and my leg," she said gaily as we sped by green-dotted hills, dramatic billows of white clouds scudding across the blue sky over our heads.

It was a glittering June day. The little church rose up before us, its light-brown suede exterior basking in the sun. Like all of the old chapels we'd seen, it looked slightly melted, askew, like a sandcastle washed by one primordial wave, then left to bake for four hundred years. Resident Indians had revered a long-buried stream there as a source of miraculous healing. Just as a chain store might spring up across the street from a popular independent, the Catholic church settled its large posterior comfortably down on the spot, started booking Virgin appearances, and took over the distribution rights. Now, dirt taken from the floor of the chapel is credited with healing powers, and thousands of pilgrims visit yearly.

Stepping through the ancient wooden doors and onto the smooth-worn, wide-planked floor was like shoving our heads into mildewed black-velvet hoods. Ninety outside, here it was cool and musty as the bottom of a well. I smelled dirt, or clay. The flickering candles at the front—masses of spilt-over wax and dusty glass votives—looked like 2:00 A.M.

at some ancient cocktail lounge. Scattered *retablos*, colonial-era folk-art portraits of saints on wooden panels, were the tipsy patrons. A carved and painted crucifix lurched from the wall high above the altar, his eyes blinking in the shivering candlelight, as if he too had just stepped in from the glare. A shadowy mix of tourists and old Latina women sat on the couple of rows of pews, or knelt at the altar. Had any of them walked or crawled all the way here on their knees for extra mileage points, as Martha had told us many did?

To the left was a squat doorway: I idly registered the *Watch Your Head* sign and bashed mine as I slouched into a narrow grotto full of Jesus doll-babies, yard-gnome Virgins, and St. Francis statues. It was like a dirty storage locker, or a hunting lodge with mounted limbs instead of boars' heads and deer antlers. One wall was lined with painted icons, cheap plastic bearded-Jesus/baby-Jesus 3-D pictures, graduation photos, typed and hand-written thank-you notes, and unidentifiable clutter; the other was lined with crutches, leg braces, false limbs, eyeglasses, and dentures left behind by those precipitously cured of whatever had brought them there. It wasn't just the baby doll in a stained satin prom dress lying on its back with its arms raised *come hither*—in a glass box of the sort usually piled with stuffed toys in bars, where you pay a quarter to try and grab one with a pair of mechanical claws that gave the fusty room a carnival air. Instinctively, I felt for my wallet.

Earlier, at Doodlets, a toy and folk-art shop a few blocks from the town square in Santa Fe, I had tenderly fingered the tin and silver limbs and organs—*milagros*, miracles. Giant tin hands and torsos, tiny silver lungs, eyes, feet; a heart like a turnip sprouting blood; cheerfully macabre and profoundly hopeful, they fairly hummed with import. They made the body sympathetic and lovable in each of its parts. *One thing at a time,* they seemed to say.

"Through there," Martha whispered now, pointing to a rounded hobbit-doorway at the front corner of the narrow room. Shouldn't she be handing us a bottle labeled *Drink Me* to translate us more properly through the telescoping spaces? I went on my hands and knees through the keyhole after Richard's disappearing bottom and feet. I felt like I was fetching a lost pet from the crawl space beneath an old house. I had that same slightly panicky feeling of knowing I could only back out the way I'd come in. It was cold and dank as a cave. A cluster of red-glass votives flickered around a simpering Mary statue, who seemed to be batting her eyelashes. There was an artless gash in the floor with a suspiciously high and loosened pile of red earth spilling out. ("They have to bring it in from outside and bless it," Martha noted back in the car, without comment.) I suppressed a hiccup of laughter. There was something both earnest and furtive in the way Richard quickly spooned dirt into the suddenly noisy shopping bag. I had no idea what he was thinking. Somebody was nudging impatiently at the back of my thighs, pushing after us into the cramped bowel. I felt I was breathing the dirt itself in the airless tank; the guardian Mary seemed to twitch with impatience. At the precise moment my scalp itched and I erupted with a violent sneeze, an overheated votive shattered with a shot, as if the Mother of God had curtly snapped her fingers. I jostled my way back out into the first grotto to lock eyes with a dirty Kewpie in a tiara housed in a tiny phone booth.

"You take that back to your room and try rubbing a little on your face," Martha told Richard. My handsome lover's most recent affliction was a Jobian outbreak of molluscum sores on his brow and drawn cheeks. ("Do I look sick?" he asked me at least once a day. "*No*," I said.) And I believe he did try a little, without discernable results. The pink bag ended up on a crowded shelf back home, till his Siamese cats Rocky and Smokey seized and batted it around the apartment one day and the miracle dirt disappeared between the couch cushions and floorboards.

What would I have left behind on Chimayó's trophy wall? Any remaining caution, maybe, about getting involved again, knowing either of us could start at any time down the road of illness and treatments and death on our hands and knees. That we had found each other at all, that I had the love of someone like Richard, whether for three years or thirty; that, back at the tiny adobe guesthouse on Canyon Road later that afternoon, waking from lovemaking and a nap to the aftermath of the daily five minute downpour and the drenched odors of *chamisa* and sage, sitting in white plastic chairs in a walled garden under a sky starkly, vastly blue once more, he could lay his hand on my leg and say, "I don't know when I last felt so happy," before Mary or whoever grew bored with upholding him only six months later and looked the other way: still miraculous.

Suddenly

Funny, the way religious nutcases come out of the woodwork
to assail you when life's dealt you a low blow, like sharks to a
shipwreck. For years it seemed as if I couldn't walk down
Bush Street to the bars on Polk looking grim or wistful or
just daydreaming without some Scientologist offering me a
free personality inventory, or a too-friendly Moonie stepping
into my path: "Hi! Want to come to our house for dinner?"

When Jack nearly died in the hospital, I would come
back to his room with a cup of coffee or the grape Popsicle
he'd requested, to find a priest or rabbi or elderly black lady
with a pamphlet leaning on his bed, persistent as the wheeling buzzards in a *Nature* episode, Jack weakly rolling his
eyes: "Get rid of her!" I know pure goodness exists somewhere, but there's an army of recruiters out there who realize they haven't got much to sell to the quick and happy, who
stick "I told you so" in a prayer and aim their sucker punch

Suddenly

at the sick, dying, and dazed with grief.

I was pretty dazed after Richard went to the hospital with pneumocystis and died, suddenly, from a "rare" toxic reaction to pentamadine. (Take it from me: if a scared-looking Kaiser intern suggests putting your lover "temporarily" on a respirator "till we see what's causing this thing," raise a fuss.) Died *suddenly*. That means, one week he was making my dachshund sing and throwing off the bedcovers with his customary, "It's *tea* time!" and the next he was somewhere in a storage room at Daphne Funerals in a $14.99 HIV body bag awaiting his turn in what the salesperson referred to as "this crazy holiday backup."

I've come to regard *suddenly* with a kind of terrified awe, as if it were some Aztec god requiring torn-out fingernails and live hearts. Suddenly makes you inclined to put off going to the dentist or painting your bathroom indefinitely. Suddenly the giant windshield wipers on a MUNI bus unmistakably mimic the obscene suck-clunk of the respirator in ICU. Suddenly rises up from the jostling obits dragging its train of stunned faces. Suddenly becomes something more than a word once you've seen close-up how abruptly one's unmade bed, half-read book, and last pair of dirty socks can be turned into artifacts in an aching tomb.

Richard's sudden end was the second time I'd lost a lover to HIV. When all my friends at work signed a card and collected memorial donations, again, I had to think of that Oscar Wilde line about how losing one parent is tragic, but losing two looks like carelessness. At about this same time— December '92—a new wave of those MTV-ish *BE HERE FOR THE CURE* billboards and bus placards went up, and I'd be crammed onto a MUNI car on my way to work with

one staring me in the face, thinking how it was a bit like reading a *Watch for Sudden Drop* sign on the wall of an elevator
shaft as you whizzed by.

I'd stopped crying all the time; stopped playing the
video of Richard crooning to Henry, just to have the ugly
thrill of seeing the actual dog listen intently and look terribly
confused. Still, sympathy—kindness of any sort—was dangerous, and I dreaded those pastel-enveloped Hallmark cards
waiting on the hall floor whenever I'd come slogging in.

One day there was one I couldn't place from the post-
mark—a small envelope, pale blue. North Texas? I'd already
heard from my younger brother in Dallas. When I saw the little bears and the word *God,* I realized Aunt Jody had somehow heard my news and felt compelled to clue me in on her
breathless prayer-life after a fifteen-year silence.

I'd last heard from Aunt Jody in 1977. I'd written a note
about my move to San Francisco, breezily mentioning that
"as you may have figured out, I'm gay, and this is the place
to be." Shortly after that I got what became known as "The
Poppycock Letter," which I read aloud at parties for years, till
it fell apart. Jody, notorious in my family for her cheesy per-
sonalized homemade gifts, had sent me back a taco-shaped
piece of clear plastic with my name painted on it in gold-
enamel script (letter holder? doorstop? part of some missing
whole?), along with a sampler can of a product then
unknown to me: Poppycock, a nasty snack of caramel-coated
popcorn and peanuts her kids were probably selling door to
door to fund a trip to the Holy Land.

"Recently, you wrote me a very frank letter. I am
responding to you equally frankly when I tell you that, as a
Christian and believer in Jesus Christ, I cannot condone or

accept your choice of lifestyle. The choice you have made is not a mere preference, as one might have for chocolate over vanilla ice cream."

It went on in this vein for a while, until Jody, the busy mother and housewife, sighed, "The children are reaching for ever-new vistas, and I've miles to go before I sleep." (Meaning she had laundry to fold, I guess. She liked to remind you she'd been a sophomore English teacher for a couple of years.) "Now the ball's in your court."

There were many balls in my court at that time, and I was easily talked out of sending her the withering reply I'd meant to by my mother, who was mortified I'd come out to one of her relatives. "Dear Aunt Jody," I'd wanted to write, "Thanks for the Poppycock. After a long afternoon of nipple play, piercing, and anal sex, me and the guys really enjoyed it."

Jody was a classic seventies Jesus freak. She was insecure and she had bad skin—she'd had a horrible childhood of constant cortisone shots for eczema. And she'd been stuck with growing up alongside my Aunt Janet, three years her junior, who was smart without studying and effortlessly pretty (her hair held a perfect *That Girl* flip), enduring endless tactless remarks about how little alike they looked, for sisters.

I remember Jody later on, as a "with it" young married woman at our big family Christmas in 1969, the year so many girls with perfectly good hair of their own were wearing silver Dynel wigs, or long horsey falls with shocking-pink or paisley bandeaux; my aunts and mother kept coolly swapping coifs in the middle of conversations. Jody was particularly pompous that year, talking down to Randy and me about the war, fancying herself earnestly "rapping" in her Central Dallas High English-teacher mode.

Kevin Bentley

Jody got born again about the time she and Uncle Tim began to try so desperately to have a baby, covering all bases with prayer *and* fertility drugs. After they'd adopted several babies, Jody mysteriously began conceiving after all. They ended up with six kids, and she found her pulpit.

The last time I'd seen her in person, I was nineteen and had driven my gaga grandmother from El Paso to Dallas so she could stay with Jody for the summer. A typical gay nineteen-year-old El Pasoan, I'd been busily cutting my Ed Psych courses, smoking dope, and popping Darvon swiped from Grandma's super stash. (If you took two, drank a beer, and sunbathed a few hours, your skull started to itch.) I'd also been staying out all night with GIs from nearby Fort Bliss. I still have the Greater Dallas-Fort Worth street map that, with pupils the size of quarters, I asked Aunt Jody to mark with the best freeway routes to all the "used-book stores" I wanted to visit—actually gay bar locations I'd culled from a borrowed *Damron Guide.*

After the Poppycock letter I didn't hear from Jody again, and the occupational-therapy gifts stopped—which meant I never got that Jesus mosaic, crafted from various dried beans and corn, she sent the rest of the family. From time to time I'd see a photo of her smiling brood grouped in front of the huge *JESUS* letters carved from redwood burl, or maybe a piece of the Ark, over their mantle, Jody aging in some pert puffed-sleeved Sears Miss fashion, the kids getting old enough to warrant my speculation as to which one—or two—was going to kick over the traces and come howling out of the closet in a few years.

The sympathy card had two fuzzy, neutered teddys embracing as if Snuggle Soft had met his other half in some leather daddy's back pocket, beneath the whimsical caption, *A Friend Is a Hug from God*. I recognized the seventh-grade-diary cursive writing. "I'm sorry you lost your friend." (More carelessness. Oh well, it was only a nameless, genderless friend, after all.) "I thought of you as I was praying yesterday. I pray God will bring you wisdom, grace, and completeness in Him."

I thought then of something Richard had told me, how back in Kentucky, when he was young and wild, he and his best friend Phil (a.k.a. Phyllis Ann, a.k.a. Fearless), would be about to tuck into their food at some HoJo's or Denny's at 2:00 A.M., and one would say, "Who'll say grace?" and they'd both shriek "Graaaace!" as if scolding some drunken woman by that name.

I thought of the Sunday morning a gaggle of Jehovah's Witnesses queued up at the top of the front stairs, interrupting our newspaper and sweet rolls, Richard saying, "You wouldn't dare, you better not," as I filled a big pot with water and sloshed it out the second-floor window, making such a resounding smack on the sidewalk that the stony-faced intruders broke ranks and rushed yelling up the block.

When Jack died, it took a long time. Death really had to walk up and down his back (a ploughed field of bedsores), flay the skin off him, and stomp on his fingers to get him to let go. The last night, as I sluiced the liquid morphine down his throat with a big dropper as the doctor had instructed me, a barely identifiable word would slip through with a moan now and then—mostly, "Please!" as in, "Get me out of this bed, get me out of here!" or "Jesus!" like you'd say it if you hit your finger with a hammer.

I thought of the snapshot I'd seen not long ago from a

family gathering for my cousin's funeral—everyone around the breakfast table in pajamas and robes. There was Jody, looking very strange. I had to think a minute before I got it: no eyebrows! Her eyebrows always did look strictly lined-on, like Myrna Loy's or Jean Harlow's. She hadn't drawn them on yet.

I thought about Jody facing the world behind her home-made eyebrows and her bossy prayer-lingo—still the ugly sister on her high horse. *Jesus!* I wished her wisdom, grace, and a complete set of facial hair.

Moon of
Monakoora

*The middle age of buggers is not to be contemplated with-
out horror.* —The Diary of Virginia Woolf: Volume 2

*Well, at my age you can't lean against a palm tree and
sing "Moon of Monakoora."* —Dorothy Lamour, on
her appearance as a sloppily dressed housewife who
gets murdered in *Creepshow 2*, quoted in her obituary

In the early eighties I used to see this older guy dancing by himself at the End-Up. He was *old*—white hair; lined, leathery
skin—and wore only a leather vest and a ripped pair of cutoffs.
He'd be waving two large Japanese fans, entirely at odds with
the disco beat. He'd stop now and then to open and inhale
from a bottle of poppers, or to blow inanely on a whistle.
Dancing Bear, we called him, snickering, recalling the stiff-
legged character in a furry suit who'd come out periodically and

177

sashay wordlessly to some cracked polka on *Captain Kangaroo.*
"Shoot me if I ever come to that, will you?" my friend
Michael would say—pretty, boyish, shaggy-blond-haired
Michael, dubbed Little Michael, because of his height and his
appearance on Polk Street when he was only sixteen. Or, he'd
croon in his best Peggy Lee manner: "She stayed too long at
the fair."

I hope to God I have something better to do by then, I'd say
to myself. Something better meaning, presumably, a devoted
lover, a real job, and a nice apartment with room for a big
rolltop desk at which I'd sit typing out poems and stories, too
happy and satisfied for drunken ennui in dance bars.

"I just hate it that you've chosen such an unhappy
lifestyle," my mother would groan each Saturday, when she
phoned from Texas. Marrying my childish father and bearing
three sons hadn't been such a jolly lifestyle choice for her, as
it happened: my parents bickered, and each son disappointed.
My older brother went to prison. I took drugs and fled to San
Francisco to be a professional homosexual. My younger
brother skipped the drugs, but refused to go to college or stay
married. My mother counted the days till she could retire
from elementary-school teaching, where she hated the kids,
and then hunkered down in misery with my half-mad father
behind the bars he'd installed on the windows and doors of
their ranch house, till she died abruptly a year later.

My thoughts fall into elementary-school addition and
subtraction: Twenty-seven years since I came to San
Francisco; sixteen years since Jack died; twelve years since
Richard died. Twenty-one years since I seroconverted.

The "older" men I went with in my first years out are
now, if they're still alive, in their early sixties. I tote up their

ages: sixty-one, sixty-five. I'm now older than either of my two lovers were when they died. They've morphed into younger men smiling out at me from the photos, as if they'd taken off on one of those light-years-long space missions and come back still in their primes to find me grown grandfatherly in gravity-driven Earth years.

A man I had an affairette with at twenty two, a handsome, urbane New York Jewish photographer, whose age awed me—thirty-nine—used to say wistfully of the gay bike messenger boys pogoing at the Stud on Punk Night, "They just don't *see* me. I'm invisible."

"What am I, a potato?" I'd think to myself, bitterly. Frank came to meet me once at Bonanza Inn Books, dressed for a job interview in black jeans, a vest and tie, a vintage sports jacket, and a rather alpine hat. "Your boyfriend's out front," a woman I worked with told me. "He's cute. Very dapper." The word lodged: one could be middle-aged, and yet *dapper*.

On my first trip to a gay ghetto, in Dallas, Texas, at nineteen, I went home not with the hunky young truck driver beside whom I'd stood most of the evening (who'd muttered to me smuttily about whether I wanted to come out to his rig and try some of the things he'd heard queers were willing to do), but with a fussy, skinny, hand-cream-scented older gentleman, who had swooped down on me as I started out of the bar. His house was a prettily restored Edwardian: glass tinkled from curio cabinets and tasseled lamps swayed like seaweed in a current as we stepped through the door and onto the echoing hardwood floor. I inhaled mildew and furniture polish. Were these the odors of forbidden sex?

He wanted the lights out before he whisked off his clothes. He dove under the sheets. I slowly pulled off my

Dingo boots and tight jeans and turned toward the bed. Standing there in the moonlight that poured through the high, lace-curtained windows, dick sticking straight up, I trembled with excitement at my first *trick*.

"Stay there a minute," he said. "Let me just look at you. You're like a Beardsley satyr." He began to explain who Beardsley was, assuming I didn't know, and I accepted my role: young and dumb. His penis was small and only partially erect. Motionless, he ejaculated with a sigh when I bent to take it in my mouth. "Sorry," he said. "I have a very short fuse." Then I lay back with my arms behind my head, while he blew me till I came.

Fifty: I picture gray-mustached men with that matronly roundness continuing below their belts, cheeks and noses ruddy with broken blood vessels, peering over their cocktail glasses behind the plate glass of the Twin Peaks (a.k.a. the Glass Coffin). Sure, Ned Rorem goes on looking great, but look what he started with.

You can get fat, or stop thinking of your choice of clothing each morning as "outfits," but if you never were a heart-stopping beauty in the first place, if you were never an Alan Helms or AMG model, you don't really have to worry about *losing your looks*.

For an oral history project, I once spoke with a seventy-seven-year-old gay man about his experiences in Nebraska in the late thirties. He told me about a cabal of "straight" pillars of the community, married doctors and lawyers, who used to rent hotel rooms in Omaha on weekends to entertain college boys—including my subject, Franklin—and street trade. The older men played poker and drank; the boys drank the free liquor and stripped down to their underwear in the summer heat. Late in the evening, the youths would have sex with each other on a couch pulled into the center of the room, while the men drank and watched, shouting encouragement, as if ringside at a fight. Then the hosts would each choose a student or farm boy or street tough with a pretty uncut dick and suck him off.

Franklin soon ceased to be *trade* ("This year's jam is next year's jelly—"), but he continued to introduce curious and comely young men from his circle to the weekend bacchanals. Certain "traditions" were instilled. He was taught how to mix a proper scotch and soda. He was never allowed to pay for a drink or dinner. "Oh no," the older gentlemen would say, covering his hand as he reached for his wallet. "You'll do that later."

1977: Attending a fund-raiser dance at California Hall, I wandered with my pal Steve into a dark room where porn movies were being screened. We squeezed down an aisle and sat on a rickety bench. I hadn't seen much homerotic film yet at that point, and I was riveted. The person on the other side of me moved right up close. I scrunched nearer to Steve, whispering "Move down!" in his ear. The unwelcome suitor followed. I glared at him: an elderly Latino fellow, wearing his black windbreaker over his head like a mantilla. When his hand darted into my crotch, I leapt to my feet in outrage. "Keep your fucking hands off me!" I hissed, and pushed my way angrily out of the room. Steve caught up with me at the bar where I was shakily ordering a Bud.

"Do you have *any* idea who that *was?*" he asked. Steve had just started his first bartending job at a sad little Tenderloin alcoholics' dive called Googie's, and he'd undergone a crash course in Royal Court genealogy. "That just so happens to have been the Dowager Empress Manuel!" He was aghast at my breach of court etiquette.

"I don't care if it was Princess Matchabelli, he didn't

have any right to grab my dick!"

Steve, ten years older, gave me his patient you're-*so*-young look: "You'll be old one day yourself, you know."

"Yeah, well, I won't be going around pawing twenty-one-year-olds and expecting them to put up with it!"

When I was eighteen, I wrote a fan letter to John Rechy after reading *City of Night*. Rechy was from my home town, El Paso, and he graduated in the top ten of his class at El Paso High alongside my mother. I was six when, on our weekly visit to the neighborhood library branch, she hurried me past a display stack of *City of Night*, murmuring, "I knew him in school. He was *strange*." The jacket art showed a slender man silhouetted against a wet, midnight street, neon and car lights reflected in the puddles like Christmas tree lights in a poorly exposed color slide. My mother didn't say the word *homosexual* then, and I wouldn't have known what it meant—but the book and the image on it reached out to me. Later, when I bought and read a worn Grove paperback with an enigmatic phone number penned inside the back cover, I knew, despite the dated and grim scenario, I was reading about a place I meant to go. The phone number was disconnected when I screwed up my nerve to call, so instead I wrote the author, thinking he might like to hear that one of his classmates had borne him an heir; I enclosed some giddy poems. He answered with a friendly letter, informing me that he was hard at work on the screenplay for *City*, and inviting me to drop by his L.A. home should I find myself in the neighborhood. I saw him a few years back in an *Advocate* spread, still in his Black Bart garb—tight black jeans, open black shirt, and cowboy boots—muscular and proud, but fragile-looking too, like the Diane Arbus shot of Mae West in her negligee. When will my Levi's, Gap T-shirts, and high-tops render me as anachronistic as a flapper?

Tradition provides a number of appropriate names for the use of middle-aged gay men in addressing their youthful counterparts: Lochinvar, Youngman, Handsome, Apollo, Sport, *Paolo*.

"You're thirty-seven? I'm thirty-two. That makes me the younger one—so I guess I'll be getting my way." This was uttered with a weary sigh at the predictable sameness of all romances, and the first of many shrugs. We were lying on the rug in my living room, books, photos, and glasses of wine spread around us. In the breaks between our kissing and pawing each other, I was trying to talk Matt into having sex on this, our first, solo date. "Of course, I'm attracted to you, but maybe this isn't a good idea." His show of reluctance ought to have put me off, along with his conviction that five years' age difference gave him a perpetual trump, but the possiblity of having sex again after four months of grief and celibacy was irresistible. I knew from past experience that nothing helped put loss into perspective faster than a good dose of sex. I'd endured one very miserable year between Jack's dying and my meeting Richard, and I felt no compunction about skipping a semester at misery school this time. I didn't want to be like my friend Nate's neighbor Sal, whose new lover everyone referred to as Sea Monkey Boyfriend (recalling those add-water seahorses advertised in comic books), because Sal met and moved in with him only weeks after Andy died. Still, a week, a month, a year—when you've watched lovers die, when you're infected and asymptomatic with no idea when HIV may dissolve the earth beneath your feet and suck you under—what's the difference, really?

Three months and innumerable *Dark Shadows* videos

later, when Matt, cigarette drooping from the corner of his downturned mouth, shrugged and lectured me one more time about sex being merely another bodily function, like going to the bathroom or blowing your nose, reading aloud a maddening passage from French feminist-deconstructionist Luce Irigaray that cast my penis obsession in a sickly light, I realized he'd been right: this wasn't a good idea. I walked away and steeled myself for the long haul.

It was a tough wait for the next good thing. *This is it, toots,* I'm thinking, *you've had all yours and you don't get any more.* Attending a revival of *West Side Story* on my fortieth birthday, I realized, as Tony and Maria sang "Tonight," that for as long as I could remember, when I read about or saw young lovers, one of them was always *me.* An unpleasant little voice inside me was saying something about this I did not like: *That's never going to be you again, honey.*

"I can't picture the kinds of things you say now coming out of *his* mouth," Paul says of me in my twenties, after perusing my old photo albums. I'd packed all the albums and diaries into one big carton and lugged it over to his loft in the first stage of moving in. Having boxed up similar items for two dead lovers, the sight of my recorded transit gathered into one pile gave me pause. Because I've stayed put these twenty-seven years in San Francisco—because I regularly leaf back through old journals—for me, the past and present are fluid, permeable. Other than the up-close arrival of HIV in the mid-eighties, there's no obvious demarcation separating young from young-no-more. I *am* that boy, give or take ten bongs and a six-pack.

Something better to do did come along, and I tired of drinking in bars or seeing how high I could make myself and still maintain, without having to bottom out and reduce my surname to an initial. The pre-AIDS diaries do seem engineered to excite and insult me now, in my more sober domesticity, with their sheer volume of sexual contacts and offhand slurs against those past thirty-five or forty. Yet I'm precluded from fretting about middle age by the very horror itself: how can I carp about birthdays, when every day I live, whole and healthy, cheating HIV out of its next meal?

Twenty-one years of asymptomatic infection, and the good news is: you may grow old.

Am I dapper yet? Do I drool over younger men? Will I Do That Later? Will I one day pass a poster for *Spiritual Retreats for Gay Men Over Forty* without laughing? Does childlessness, sexual voracity, and a fondness for small dogs invariably lead to Wallis Simpson? Can one be elderly *and* masculine without a past in the Merchant Marine? Will my tumultuous puberty ever end? If it does, will I have Something Better to Do? I intend to find out.

Little Michael, who died young and stayed pretty—I wasn't asked to shoot him, as it turned out; he did it himself when he started to get sick—came to me in a dream a few years ago. Putting his arm over my shoulder, he told me about the rest of my life, smiling and teasing. "So don't worry," he said. "Of course, you know you can't remember any of this future stuff when you wake up. I'm not going to be coming back to talk to you anymore after this, either. I'm moving on."

He said it like he was heading to a bar, for which I was neither attractive nor young enough. But he was laughing, affectionately.

Party of Two

My lover's only long-term relationship prior to me was with not one but two other men, lasting eleven years. They'd worn matching rings, and when he amicably left the ménage, Paul had gone on wearing his till he and I bought wedding bands several years into our relationship.

"Where's your ring?" his mother asked, alone with him in the kitchen on our first trip to New Jersey after the switch.

"Kevin and I got rings, so now I'm wearing this one."

"Oh." That was all she asked, and I was surprised to hear she'd asked that much.

Paul had left home and moved to San Francisco about a month before I did, in the summer of 1977, but unlike me he remained close to his family, flying back twice a year, often at Christmas. They're a tightly knit group; Paul's sister, her husband, and their two kids live less than a mile from the modest Cape Cod his parents have owned since 1959. His folks, Sam and Josephine, first-generation Italian-Americans who've mostly forgotten the language their parents spoke, have always been popular with Paul's and Diane's friends, many of whom are gay. They loved John and Ray, who visited both with Paul and on their own when traveling to the East Coast on business. They've always been kind and accepting of me, remembering to ask after me when they call, sending birthday cards and Christmas gifts along with Paul's. They just don't say the word.

I'd joked to Paul that surely one gay lover was less awkward to explain than a three-way, but actually that had made obfuscation easy: three young men living together had to be roommates and no other explanation would ever have occurred to Lily Trucksess or Lily Myer, the widows who lived on either side of his parents, or Uncle Joe, Aunt Millie, or Cousin Jeanie.

Seeing Paul for the first time, in a photo, people say, "He has kind eyes," yet my first impression was of taciturnity or even severity—which turned out to be his response to the pressure and unpredictability of our first face-to-face meeting. That sternness, from a beefy, hairy, good-looking Italian man, activated a gut-level attraction in me that's never flagged, despite the concomitant hot temper and moodiness.

He'd been looking at the sex ads in *BAR* when his eye strayed to my *Books and Sex—are reasons to live* heading in the relationships section. This was April of '96, just before every last vestige of the hooking-up enterprise migrated to the Internet. I'd gotten a slew of muzzy voice-mail messages, with chattering ice cubes in highball glasses in the background, saying things like, "Books? I've got a few books around here if you wanna take a look at 'em..."

His phone voice was warm, with a butch New Jersey accent that at first reminded me slightly of a very hot guy I'd dated in the early eighties who ended up punching me—but minus the angry and crazy part. Though he didn't realize till we'd been talking for some time that I was HIV-positive, he didn't back away—in fact, it was only much later that he con fessed this had been a surprise. I was surprised he'd answered my ad, being negative.

We met for coffee next door to the Van Ness Avenue bookstore at which an author whose book I'd edited was to read that evening. As we sat outside with our lattes at a tippy white plastic table, my best friend Bob pulled up in his unmistakable '72 Toyota, swung into a parking space just in front of us, got out, and bustled toward the bookstore, then turned and walked back to us. "Hey," I said weakly.

"What are you doing here?" he said, looking from me to Paul. "I'm just running in to pick up something I've got on hold."

"Uh, I'm kind of on a date. This is Paul."

Paul shifted uncomfortably through the introduction and a brief conversation before Bob hurried off. "That was a setup, right?"

"Nope—total coincidence." Or "co-inkeydink," as my workmate Isaac liked to say, with that New Age twinkle in his eye that made him look like an anime, meaning "there are no accidents."

I told Paul about some of the other bachelors I'd inter-viewed so far: the pale, redheaded, forty-five-year-old gradu-ate student who'd groomed himself like a chimp (had he actually eaten that scab?) while he babbled condescendingly about his research topic ("Trust me, you wouldn't understand even if I *tried* to explain it"). I'd knocked my chair over in my haste to escape that one. And Number Two, who'd mailed me a seriously weird letter written as if from *me* to *him*, apologizing for my thoughtless behavior in deciding he—not to mention his guru, Omni Ra—wasn't for me. Now, as we wound between bookshelves on our way to the rows of metal chairs in the back of the store, I pulled my promising Bachelor Number Five aside. "If you're feeling anything like what I was with the human Gila monster, you can leave now, it's okay."

"That's not what I'm feeling," he said, pulling me into his arms.

"Life begins at forty," Drew had often said, haunting then, but it had turned out to be true for me: mine started up again when I met Paul.

At that time, Paul was a finance manager for a snack-food and cigarette distributor where the bosses were always flying off on R. J. Reynolds-hosted golf junkets and dropping Xeroxed pro-tobacco letters on employees' desks to be signed and sent off to lawmakers. I was acquiring books for a metaphysical publishing house in a downturn, being sent out to poach possible best-selling authors for our list—like the man who transmitted the Altarians, beings from another solar system that spoke through him in an Indian accent, who explained to me over an expense-account dinner how he required frequent deep-tissue work for the bite one of the lizard aliens had taken out of his neck in a past life scuffle for control of a spaceship hurtling toward Earth. "Interesting...," I'd say, topping off my wineglass. "Do you see this as a hardcover or paperback original?"

Paul and I saw each other for just under a year before I gave up my apartment and moved, with the increasingly white Henry, into his Mission District loft. His mostly modern metal, glass, and open space décor looked more like Hamburger Mary's or The Sausage Factory once my old bookcases, desk, chairs, framed vintage photos and engravings, and plant stand were wedged in and jostling the brushed-nickel dining chairs and coffee table. My mismatched pots, pans, dishes, and silverware went to storage, since his were nicer; my stereo, TV, and coffeemaker were given away, cutting loose the lifeboats. I changed jobs, he changed jobs. We got another miniature dachshund, Oscar, to keep Henry lively in his old age. We got to know each other's friends. He found out my faults: I don't like to drive anymore, I'd rather rent the DVD six months later than go to the movies, I can't read with the TV on, I snore. I got to know his: dissatisfaction with our loft and not being able to afford a house in San Francisco; exasperation with the smallest things, from traffic to spots on the carpet; the way, once I moved in, he stopped thinking absolutely everything I said or did was charming and delightful. (In those early days he'd prop his head on his arm and stare at me in bed, repeating my name in wonder like Melvyn Douglas in *Ninotchka,* till I would have to croak, "That is my name, comrade. Why do you repeat it?") He clenched his teeth through my *Best of Melanie* CD; I stopped my ears and gabbled "Pop Goes the Weasel" to block out his Beach Boys *Pet Sounds.*

"I want it to stay romantic, and I want us to be faithful," I'd said when he first proposed moving in together. "I'm not looking for just a *life partner* to discuss my tricks with."

Luckily, he wanted that too—and the sex part just got better and better. "Whoa!" we'd say, falling back panting. "Wow, what got into you?" "Do you think there's something wrong with us to still be like this after two...four...eight years?" When it came down to it, we'd both lived through the promiscuous late seventies and eighties, we'd both lost friends and lovers (John had died two years after Paul left the relationship), we'd both spent time unhappily alone and wondering if we'd ever find someone again—and we still couldn't believe the fate or happenstance that had brought us together.

We'd brushed against each other nearly two decades before. We soon discovered that in our second year in the city we had lived in apartment buildings across from each other on Post Street, just off Polk. Later on, a name came up in an anecdote about how Paul had spent New Year's Eve in 1978. "What was that name again?" I asked.

"Leslie Green. Please, he practically wanted to marry me," Paul said. "He called me Paolo and brought me flowers." I'd been having a sporadic affair with the same man at approximately the same time, though in my case there were no pet names or posies—just cigars and rough sex. Like several other functionally bisexual men I'd known, Les married a woman and headed for the hills when AIDS came along. An idle moment's Googling turned him up, with two teenage children. "Should we send him a Christmas card?" Paul wondered.

Paul's parents used to have a condo in Florida, where Sam moved his business some years back, but now that's all been sold, and in their late seventies, they stay close to home. Sam tends his lawn and plays golf with his old business partner; Jo

Kevin Bentley

cooks and talks on the phone. They aren't prudish or judg-
mental or even terribly religious—Sam drives Jo to mass most
Sundays but only attends a couple of times a year himself;
there are some stiff Palm Sunday fronds gathering dust in the
china hutch that shimmies alarmingly when you tread on a
certain area of the dining room floor. Far from right wing,
Sam's a feisty independent, frequently holding forth on
"these people who think they got the right to tell other people how to live." The pope, Pat Robertson, and the Bush
administration set him off. "Aw, that pope! Let me tell you
somethin' about him," he'll begin, his fingers brushing his
thumbs as if conjuring a little ball of truth. Josephine is neither outspoken nor pious, just quiet and, well, normal in a
comfortable way. She worries about her family and is happiest surrounded by them.

But there's an invisible force field. They don't watch
Will and Grace because there's always something they prefer
on the other channel. If there's a gay-related story on the
news while we're all crammed into the tiny wood-paneled
den—dead silence, or a sudden burst of unrelated conversation. "Did I tell you Doris and Rusty were down the Shore?"
Jo will say, while a television announcer intones the teaser for
a *20/20* segment on gay unions. Yet on the wall behind the
TV, halfway along the left slope of the pyramid of framed
family photos—sepia prints of elderly Italian grandparents;
handsome young Sam and pretty Jo at a forties nightclub and
at their wedding; teenage Paul and Diane with unisex shags,
their graduation photos; Diane and Roger's wedding, their
two kids (Paul: "Thank God for Diane!")—there's a recent
shot of Paul and me holding our dachshunds and surrounded
by antique prints and furniture that's just three snaps short of

a rainbow tattoo. *"See?"* Paul says. "What more do you want? You're right there on the wall."

They're growing fragile: Sam can't hear and wrestles with his chirping hearing aid; Jo's heavy and holds on to countertops and furniture to move around. Sam carried a large pair of pruning shears out to the street to confront the hoodlum burning rubber in his driveway. Jo pulled in front of someone on her four-block drive to the beauty parlor and wrecked her car. Sam took an air pistol to the squirrels that were eating his bedding plants, but was talked into disarming.

At a posh restaurant for a Mother's Day celebration on one of my first visits, along with Diane, Roger, and the kids, we were waiting for our table, when the hostess approached with an armful of menus. *"Grip,* party of eight?" Sam smiled mysteriously and motioned to her.

I looked at Paul, who rolled his eyes. "It's his little joke," he said into my ear as we headed after the others. "He says it's easier than spelling Grippardi." He mimed zipping his lip.

Another year we flew to New Jersey for Paul's niece's sweet-sixteen party. I'd often seen throngs of lavishly decked-out Latina girls near a Catholic church I walk past in the Mission celebrating their *quinceanos,* but sweet-sixteen parties were not something I was familiar with. Diane had rented a large restaurant party room with a dance floor and deejay. The girls were wildly done up in formal gowns; Julie, Paul's niece, had spent the day having a tiara woven into her hairdo. Since I'd met Paul, she'd moved briskly from giggly little girl playing with Beanie Babies to cheerleader with a cell phone. The centerpiece of the evening was the candle-lighting ceremony—all sixteen of them, each introduced with a little tribute and the opening bars of songs Julie had chosen, each followed by hugs and wiping away of tears. Apparently there'd been a lot of jockeying for position in the "friends lighting candles" category right up to the last minute, but her parents', Sam and Jo's, and Paul's and mine were assured. Up we went, Uncle Paul and…Kevin, like The Captain and Tenille; since the theme snippets were all from the beginnings of songs, we lit our candle to the slightly ominous opening of "California Dreaming" where all the leaves are brown and the skies are gray.

Later, the dancing finally reached the point where boys other than Julie's limber, smartly dressed, and clearly gay pal Louis joined the girls on the parquet disco floor, and then the older guests—parents, aunts and uncles—dragged each other up and improvised whatever rock-and-roll step they'd gotten by on since the seventies. Roger and Diane were dancing, then Paul and his lesbian best friend Donna, currently single. "Don't you want to dance?" yelled Diane, returning to the table laughing and out of breath.

If I asked Paul to dance with me I'd be putting him on the spot. Everybody knew Paul was Julie's gay uncle—most of the kids have at least one, and they're very handy for trips into the city for shows—but I knew he wouldn't want to do it and I knew I couldn't bear to be told no.

It's Julie's night, I told myself. *Don't make it about you.*

There's a story my younger brother tells about my maternal grandmother, Beulah, back in Texas. She was good to us when we were little, but she'd had a hard life and had never been a happy person, and she grew increasingly ill-tempered and bigoted in her seventies and eighties. She had a lot of funny turns of speech that must have dated back to the hardscrabble cotton farm she grew up on, like "She's nothing but a whore—her dress was up to here and you could see her crack!" and "He thinks he's something on a stick!" Of most meals she'd remark sadly, "I liked it real well, but it made me sick." Of sex with our grandfather, whom she had addressed as Pa, she said succinctly, "It like to killed me." In her last days, suffering the effects of high blood pressure, a stroke, and diabetes, she was looked after during the day by home health-care aides, all heavyset young black women she insisted were stealing her cans of tuna. When Char'nay had left one evening, Grandma turned to Mark and asked, "Is she gone?"

"Yeah, Grandma," he said.

"You sure?"

"Uh-huh."

She gripped the arms of her chair and yelled the N-word till she was hoarse and gasping for air. "I been waiting all day to do that."

Sometimes on the flight back to California, or in the backseat of the cab from the airport, I have to fight a ludicrous urge to shout, "GAYGAYGAY!"

"Don't you think it's a good sign that he's close to his family?" I said to my friends when he and I first met. I worried that my alienation from my parents might follow me like a bad smell. I could have kept up more normal-*appearing* relations with my parents if I'd been willing to clam up about my "lifestyle," but the truth is the tension and unhappiness in our family unit long predated, and went way beyond, my coming out. "You and your brother have both made some bad lifestyle choices," my mother told me when Randy went to prison. For his part, Mark got married for a while and waited till after our mother died, when he was thirty-five, to come out, having seen how it went with me.

We only had maternal relatives in my family, since my father, whose own dad dropped dead of a heart attack when he was still a baby, wanted nothing to do with his mother and siblings back in Georgia. Grandma Beulah, and my grandfather, Grady, went months at a time without speaking to each other. When my mother's older sister, Joyce, got married against Grady's wishes and moved to California, he didn't speak to her till her first child was born four years later.

I had nothing to do with my father after I left home. Twelve years later, when I discovered that my mother had kept Jack's death a secret, I changed my phone number and put a stop to her weekly calls. I was powerless to resurrect Jack; here was one thing I could do to show how much I loved him, though he'd have urged just the opposite. When the birthday cards arrived I threw them in the trash.

When my mother died and my father gutted the house of her effects, from furniture to photo albums, it seemed like he was punishing her for leaving. His new wife refused to use even my mother's silverware, as if she'd died of TB, not cancer. A few years later, he was diagnosed with a rare disease and in the course of several months lost his memory, his mobility, and finally his ability to swallow. He died shortly after that, having disinherited all three sons, a cruel surprise to my younger brother, who'd remained in contact with him.

Paul had something as alien to me as life on Altaira: a happy childhood. No compulsory church after confirmation; all the meatballs, macaroni, Ring Dings and Yodels a boy could want; a posse of friends in high school who, after graduation, all turned out to be gay. Oh sure, sometimes Sam might have yelled about Diane sneaking off to New York to see Jimi Hendrix at the Filmore East or Jo might have had to flick the light switch at the bottom of the stairs for Paul to turn down the Elton John. Sure, they like to linger at the table mulling over old feuds or dishing cheap, lazy, or high-handed relatives—"I'll tell you somethin' about Uncle Tony! He don't pay for nothin' he don't have to!"—but nobody ever screams and breaks the dishes. On the first night of an East Coast stay, jet-lagged, gazing around the candlelit table at the four of them laughing and yelling over macaroni, gravy, meatballs, sausage, and *brasciole,* if I take off my glasses I see the shimmering Rushmore of their similar noses, the nimbus of light around each flushed face, and I'm pierced with envy.

Paul and Diane call their parents Mommy and Daddy to their faces and in discussing them with each other, as they frequently do, over the phone. "Mommy called me three times already this morning. You don't know what it's like!" You don't have to read the rhymed couplets in the flowery Hallmarks Paul receives for every holiday to see how much his parents adore him, all the more because they don't get to see him every day. "I can't get them to the Short Hills Mall," Diane will say, "but if King Paul wants to spend a week down the Shore, oh boy, pack up the car!"

We went back for the Thanksgiving after 9/11. Roger, a big sweet ex-biker, ex-marine, picked us up in his "staff car," a mini-pickup with flags fluttering from either front fender. "Where's our gas masks?" I wanted to know. Diane's boss, a successful sports doctor, had bought gas masks for all his employees and their family members.

"I got news for you," she said, "We were breathing it here, okay?" Diane, Paul, and Sam start sentences that way a lot: *I got news for you.*

"What is this, CNN?" I asked.

Later that evening the phone rang and I answered it— some neighbor lady asking for Paul's mom. I could hear the other woman launching into questions as I handed the phone off to Jo, and, on my way out of the kitchen, I paused. "Oh...that..." she lowered her voice "...was one of Paul's friends from California."

When Paul came upstairs later to see where I'd gone, I was lying on the uneven double bed made out of two twins pushed together, staring at the shelves of book-club editions, family snapshots in Lucite cubes, his framed first-communion photo, and the ceramic version of their late Lhasa apso, Jethro.

"I've been disappeared. I don't exist."

"C'mon, don't do this. That was Connie Thompson from two blocks over, what business is it of hers who you are?"

"If it was Roger she'd say 'that was Diane's husband, Roger.'"

"Look, what do you want me to do? They just don't have a word for it."

"They're ashamed."

"I don't want to have this conversation now."

I was a notorious sulker as a child—several early report cards document it—at school, putting my head down and refusing to speak; at home, staying shut in my room for hours on end with my fists balled, staring at the wall. "You aren't hurting anyone but yourself," my mother would sing, carrying away the dessert I'd spurned, or jingling the car keys as she and the others headed out to a movie.

In the first few months of living with Jack I learned what it means to stick with someone—to roll with the surprises instead of walking away when the other person did something I found unacceptable, as I always had with everyone else. He'd been honest about his past coke problems, but less so about having quit. The first time he walked in really fucked up—eyes bulging, stuttering, repeating, "I love ya, understand? I love ya, understand?"—I kicked the furniture and threatened to move out and didn't speak for a day. Then he sat me down and said, "Look, I'm forty years old and I've been doing as I please for a long time. You can't expect me to change overnight because you say so." And for the first time in my life, I backed down.

"Just because they don't say the word doesn't make them like *your* parents," Paul says.

The following summer I was standing in a security line at SFO with Paul's parents while he parked the car. He'd flown them out for a week with us at the weekend place that he, Ray, and John bought twenty years ago at Russian River, and it had been a happy, relaxed time. Sam sat on a bench in the front yard and threw a tennis ball for Oscar while we gardened; Jo made macaroni and gravy one night; we went for drives and watched old movies. One night Paul turned up the lights on the paneled wall behind the woodstove in the family room and explained to his parents who was who in this pyramid of framed photos—old ones of him on vacations with Ray and John, Ray with his current lover Bob, our friends Karry and Sean and their two little boys, Donna and her then girlfriend, Joanne and hers, several of us together.

After comments on the size of the airport crowd and how long Paul might take, there was some awkward silence; as it happened I'd seldom been left alone with the two of them. Jo turned toward me, looking slightly agitated. "I want you to know we consider you a member of this family," she said, her eyes filling up. Sam's back was turned; I doubted he'd heard.

I leaned over the luggage to give her a little hug. Was I embarrassed because I sensed how awkward this was for her? What was she thinking? God knows, I did want them to love me. "Thanks for telling me that," I said. And then Paul was striding up, and Sam was fretting about their tickets, and the world moved on.

In June of 2001, nine years after Richard's and my stay there, Paul and I spent a week in Santa Fe. One afternoon, we drove out to Chimayó. The chapel was smaller than I remembered, the side room less cluttered—surely they'd winnowed out some of the crutches and photos? And the height of the doorway to the little grotto: it's low, but you duck, not crawl. I peered inside and saw that the hole in the floor went straight down several feet—where was the miracle dirt? As Paul and I stood looking around the side room, a little Latina lady bustled up and plucked at my sleeve. "Are you strong enough to help me lift something?" I assumed she wanted help moving a big chair or something. "The man who usually comes to bring the dirt hasn't come," she said, matter-of-factly, and handed me a large plastic paint pail.

Oh boy! I thought. *This is really too perfect.* I cast one meaning look back at Paul and then followed her out a side door and around to the back of the chapel, where a pile of reddish dirt, half covered by a blue sheet of plastic, lay in a huge mound as if deposited there by a dump truck. By now I'd asked her name (Sister Thelma, though she wore a sort of generic skirt and blouse) and told her mine. Sister Thelma handed me a smaller pail and indicated that I should use it to scoop up dirt and fill the larger one, as well as a second big pail she pointed to. When I couldn't reach more dirt by bending, I gingerly put one foot against the pile to balance so I could reach up higher, at which point Sister Thelma said either, "Careful, you'll get dirt on your shoe," or "Don't put your shoe on the holy dirt." I had no idea which. In any case I got a dusting of the powdery earth on my blue tennis shoes. When both pails were full, she took one from me, and we set out lugging them back around the chapel. "Doesn't this have to be blessed by a priest, or do they do the whole batch ahead of time?" I asked helpfully.

"No, no," she said, waving one hand vaguely at the horizon, "everything here is holy, the rocks, the trees."

As we walked back into the side chapel, Paul gave me the look of fond bemusement that always makes me feel I'm exactly where I should be. A man with a camera waiting in line to enter the grotto turned to his companion and said snidely, "Oh look, here comes the 'holy dirt.'" Ignoring him, Sister Thelma cut in front of the line and gestured to show me how I should upend both pails to fill the little gaping hole and then, when I'd done so, dropped a beat-up gardening trowel she pulled from her pocket straight down so that it stuck in the dirt like a switchblade. "Aren't you going to take some?" she said.

And so I had a second go at the miracle dirt, just as I've gotten so many other second chances.

As I got to know Paul better, as I began to love him for reasons besides the strong physical connection and the pleasure of his company, I found myself noticing things about him— his appearance in photos; certain mannerisms, gestures, and expressions; his brusque assurance, sometimes even a way of speaking—that I recognized as astonishingly like Jack, though he differs from Jack in fundamental ways. In the same split second it takes to identify one of these utterly unique gestures or intonations, it's as if I've run some disintegrating strip of old nitrate footage, and I can no longer picture Jack doing it. Is this how love banishes grief? Sometimes I feel him moving in the next room or see the back of his head or hear him exclaim over something and, as is so often the case in dreams, I don't know which of them it is. I just know it's the one I love.

Acknowledgments

Sincere thanks for this and much more to Andrew and Liz McBeth of Green Candy Press, and to Clifford Chase for generous and insightful editing. Thanks are also due to text and jacket designer Ian Phillips, and to Tom Ace, Walter Armstrong, Scott Brassart, Robert Drake, Amy Durgan, Howard Junker, Bonnie Lesley, Michael Lowenthal, Daisy Meacham, Tim Murphy, Bruce Shenitz, David Thorpe, and Terry Wolverton.

Kevin Bentley is the author of *Wild Animals I Have Known: Polk Street Diaries and After*, and the editor of *Boyfriends from Hell: True Tales of Tainted Lovers, Disastrous Dates, and Love Gone Wrong*, both Lambda Literary Award finalists. He is also the author of *Sailor: Vintage Photos of a Masculine Icon*; and the editor of *Afterwords: Real Sex from Gay Men's Diaries*. His writing has appeared in various anthologies including *Best Gay Erotica 2003* and *The Man I Might Become: Gay Men Write About Their Fathers* and in *POZ*, *OUT Magazine*, and *ZYZZYVA*. He lives in San Francisco.

Also by Kevin Bentley
Praise for *Wild Animals I Have Known*

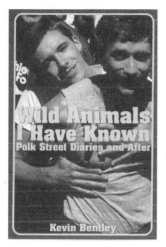

"Difficult to put down... These brief portraits of gay male egoists eventually amount to a small epic of neurotic behavior that may be endemic to pleasure meccas like San Francisco. *Wild Animals* is a graceful, sad, and very skillful tale..." —Andrew Holleran, *The Gay & Lesbian Review Worldwide*

"Bears witness to a city in the middle of an unparalleled sexual gold rush... Bentley is a natural and charming writer... never self-conscious or preening." —Chris Schmidt, *Lesbian & Gay New York*

"One part Armistead Maupin, one part Chi Chi LaRue... Offers a twinge of delightful, guilty pleasure." —Jason Dorn, *SFWeekly*

"This is the kind of book that gives promiscuity and sleaze a good name... raw, brave, brash, even witty erotica." —Richard Labonte, *Bookmarks*

"The best memoir of 1970s San Francisco published so far." —Jesse Monteagudo, *Dallas Voice*

"A fabulous emotional roller-coaster of a read." —*Out Front Colorado*

To read an excerpt visit www.greencandypress.com